handywoman's
workbook

handywoman's
workbook

how to do it yourself without breaking a nail

Bridget Bodoano

Quadrille

Editorial Director: Jane O'Shea
Creative Director: Mary Evans
Art Director: Helen Lewis
Designers: Katy Davis and Jim Smith
Project Editor: Lisa Pendreigh
Text Editor: Nicki Marshall
Special Photographer: Graham Atkins Hughes
Picture Research: Nadine Bazar
Illustrators: Bridget Bodoano and Coralie Bickford-Smith
Production: Tracy Hart

First published in 2002 by Quadrille Publishing Limited
Alhambra House
27–31 Charing Cross Road
London WC2H OLS

Cataloguing-in-Publication Data: a catalogue record for this book is available
from the British Library.

ISBN 1 903845 39 4

Printed and bound in Singapore

contents

introduction

The traditional division of labour with men putting up shelves while grateful women clean up the mess now seems quaint as well as decidedly politically incorrect. There is plenty of evidence that today's women are putting up their own shelves – and that men are discovering the joys of housework.

The enormous increase in the number of single households means that a large proportion of women have no 'man about the house' and so must remain shelf-less unless they are prepared to Do It Themselves. Of course, many women have perfectly nice men around the house but not all of them are keen on DIY or any good at it – after all, insisting that all men are naturally handy with a hammer is as politically incorrect as

suggesting that women should stick to dusting. Others, tired of standing by their man, dutifully passing the tape measure, drill, wallplugs, screws and screwdriver have taken the comparatively small step to using the tools themselves.

However, while the numbers of women getting involved in DIY is rising steadily there are still a lot of modern, emancipated ones who, though they can simultaneously programme a mobile phone and download a complicated system onto a computer, have yet to come to grips with a hammer or a power drill. Equally, the old-fashioned, pipe-smoking, shed-inhabiting Dad in a jumper who once would have taken pride in teaching his offspring the best way to hold a chisel has been replaced by modern, denim-

clad Dad, much too busy tinkering with his sound system or his motorbike to be bothered with brackets and bradawls.

The old image of DIY as a 'hobby', with enthusiasts spending every weekend ruining perfectly nice homes with inappropriate, unwise, unattractive and unsuccessful DIY, has been replaced with a new sexier image for DIY which is all about making the best of your home and creating a personal space to suit your needs as well as your personality and particular passions.

The new look for modern interiors is essentially simpler and pared down with the emphasis on the space and the structural qualities of a room or building. Achieving this often involves taking out the previous occupants out-dated, tatty attempts at home 'improvements' in order to restore calm and dignity to abused properties.

The advice and information in this book is intended to encourage you to use basic tools and skills to repair and prepare your home for inspired decoration and stylish additions! The decorating techniques are intended to encourage and inspire you to tackle simple projects and perhaps consider more major improvements to your home.

Doing It Yourself is not only very satisfying but you also benefit from knowing that the job has been done properly – often at a fraction of the cost of employing a professional. However, not all jobs are suited to beginners and some should only be carried out by a regis-

tered expert. By learning something of the wonders and mysteries hidden behind walls and under floors, and the sorts of problems that can arise when carrying out repairs and improvements, you will be able to judge whether to have a go yourself or whether it might not be better to leave it to the experts.

cool kit

the essential guide to tools and materials

Shopping for tools can be as pleasurable as shopping for clothes with the added bonus that, in comparison, everything seems such a bargain. For the price of a designer label T-shirt you can buy a whole toolkit that will last for years, won't shrink in the wash and won't go out of fashion. Power tools are a lot cheaper than power dressing and you can varnish a whole floor for the price of a decent manicure.

The ambience of a large DIY store may not be quite as stylish as a high-street shop but it has a buzzy, busy atmosphere. First visits can be a bit daunting, but many stores have a policy of providing plenty of staff willing to guide you through a job and advise on the tools and equipment needed to carry it out. In fact, in the world of DIY there is no shortage of advice. Make friends with the staff in your local builders' merchant or hardware store. Faced with serving grumpy builders for most of the day, they will be only too happy to explain how, why and what to buy – and may throw in a few good jokes and the odd discount as well.

Many of the large DIY stores cater mainly for the amateur enthusiast. They have all the products that make the jobs easier with tools, fittings and ready-cut materials that make it possible for non-professionals to tackle quite ambitious projects. Many stores also produce very good how-to leaflets that give detailed and responsible instructions along with clear drawings and useful tips. However, some of the easy-to-do solutions lead to less than stylish results, so be discriminating in your choice of materials. Keep to simple jobs using good-quality, good-looking components.

Choosing which tools and materials to buy is made very difficult by the widely differing prices for what, at first glance, seem to be very similar products. For items such as basic hand tools the quality will be reflected in the price: for a beginner the cheaper ones are usually perfectly adequate. For anything that involves machinery, motors or electricity it is better to go for a well-known, reputable brand as they will conform to the required standards and safety regulations. Own-brand decorating materials are often much cheaper; many of them are extremely good value and do not differ greatly from the well-known brands. However, some cheap paints are often thinner and therefore need extra coats, while products such as fillers are just not as good as the more expensive versions. Trial and error is one way to find out but don't be afraid to ask staff or even other shoppers. There is a matey camaraderie amongst DIYers that can lead to enlightening conversations in the plumbing aisle or even long-term relationships!

10 basic hand tools

There are a huge number of fancy and frightening looking tools on the market, but most basic DIY jobs can be done with a select few. The difficult part is deciding which of the hundred or so screwdrivers hanging on the DIY store racks is the one for you. Good quality is important, but expensive tools are usually for professionals or picky purists. There are many perfectly good tools at very reasonable prices.

bradawl

A short, sharp spike sticking out of a chunky handle. Used for marking the position and making a small pilot hole for nails, screws and hooks.

cutting knife

The classic cutting knife has a chunky, easy-to-grip handle with strong replaceable blades that come in a variety of shapes. Used for cutting everything from cardboard to carpet.

spirit level

An intriguing device that shows whether surfaces and edges are truly horizontal and vertical. Vital for putting up shelves.

claw hammer

No tool kit is complete without one. Used for knocking in nails, but more frequently for taking them out. Invaluable for minor demolition work.

tape measure

A metal retractable tape measure can be used for measuring rooms or marking out smaller distances. A medium-width 3m (10 ft) long tape measure will fit nicely in your hand.

try square

Consists of a rectangle of wood with a rectangle of metal set into it at exactly 90 degrees. Useful for marking lengths of wood, cutting and checking right angles.

screwdrivers

There are two main types: the cabinet, which has a flat tip and is used for screws with a straight slot in the head, and the cross-point which is used for screws with a cross-shaped slot. You will need both types which come in various sizes and lengths. For faster screwing there are power screwdrivers. They save energy and screw tighter, and in reverse gear their other great function is undoing screws.

spanners

For tightening, and undoing, nuts and bolts. Adjustable spanners can be altered to fit any size bolt but are a bit fiddly. A set of spanners isn't too expensive.

saws

Buy an all-purpose saw for cutting wood, metal and plastics. Also invest in a small hack-saw with a thin, replaceable blade which is useful for cutting metal and plastic pipes.

pliers

For gripping objects so that you can turn, squeeze, pinch or pull out a variety of things from nails in awkward corners to screw tops that won't unscrew. They usually have a hole in the centre with a blade for cutting wire. Blunt-nose pliers are good for general use but the long-nose variety are useful for fiddly things.

10 tool tips

Treat yourself to a smart box or bag with compartments or pockets to store your tools.

Make sure your toolkit is easily accessible.

Always put tools back in their box or bag once you have finished with them.

Keep any instructions for use with the tools.

Buy a power drill that comes in a handy bag with storage for all its kit.

Keep all sharp blades covered when not in use.

Carefully throw away all old disposable blades.

Always keep a pair of rubber gloves, goggles, a mask and some plasters in your toolkit.

Keep a set of screwdrivers and spanners together in their original packaging or in a natty pocketed roll.

For a safe and comfortable grip, always choose power tools that fit your handsize and are not too heavy.

girl power

Power tools are a great boon to anyone keen on DIY. Although these weapon-like objects may look a bit frightening, they are surprisingly easy to use providing you choose one that is suited to your capabilities and stature. What can be difficult is choosing which ones to buy. The variety of power tools on offer range from screwdrivers to large circular saws, with a few snazzy multifunction options in between. They come in a variety of shapes, sizes and colours but don't be guided by looks – some of the best-looking are low-powered or only designed for specialist tasks.

The range of tools on offer in most DIY stores is large whilst information is scarce, so do a little research first. Browsing through catalogues and the internet is a good way to discover the function, power and speed of products. Many companies offer a helpline where assistants dispense the right sort of advice (and don't mind in the least if you don't know your chuck from your elbow).

getting tooled up

There are several tempting-looking power tools on the market, but initially try to resist buying anything other than a power drill. Planers, circular saws and belt sanders need a higher level of skill and can always be hired if necessary. A jigsaw, however, is not too difficult to use and will give a neater, straighter cut than a handsaw, and with a lot less effort.

For starters, invest in a power drill: you won't be able to make holes in solid walls without one. Today, even the most basic power drill possesses many properties that were once only available on professional trade models including high power, variable speed, hammer action and reverse gear. Very often they can be used as screwdrivers and a range of accessories can be added for sanding and polishing.

Motor power is expressed in watts: the higher the wattage the more powerful and versatile the drill. They usually range from 500W to 1000W; you will need around 700W to 800W if you want to drill into masonry. Low-powered drills don't usually have hammer action (see below).

Hammer action allows for easy drilling into hard surfaces. A simple rotary action is sufficient for making holes in wood, but for masonry a hammer or percussion action (which adds vibration as well as rotation) is necessary. Most new drills feature both and selection is made with a switch or button.

The ability to vary the speed allows for more efficient drilling: most modern drills now have this facility. Speed is given in revs per minute and most general-purpose drills will go up to 3000 rpm. Slower speeds are needed for drilling into particularly hard surfaces, and faster speeds are used for wood to give a neat finish and prevent splitting. Most modern drills have variable speed control allowing you to set a speed suited to the material being drilled. A slow speed is also necessary if you want to use the drill as a screwdriver. Reverse is essential if you are going to use the drill to remove as well as drive screws. It also comes in handy if the drill bit gets stuck.

powering ahead

Power tools are driven by either electricity direct from the mains (corded) or by battery (cordless). Cordless drills were developed for use in places where putting in a plug can be difficult or dangerous, such as outside or up a tall ladder. While cable-free drilling is undoubtedly convenient, there are disadvantages. With a battery the power is not consistent – it will lessen as the battery runs down – and it can be a bit of a drag remembering to re-charge it. Buy a spare battery and keep it on charge so it's ready for use when the first battery goes flat. Something that plugs in is usually just as convenient but be aware of the cable: don't get entangled in it and, if it is too short to allow free movement, use an extension lead.

boring facts

When drilling, the part that actually makes the hole is called a bit. Bought separately, the bit fits into the drill chuck (a ring of claws that grip the bit firmly) which is then tightened.

If the drill has a keyed chuck the tightening is done with a chuck key. The key fits into three holes on the chuck and is turned until it won't go any further (you need to tighten it in all three holes). A keyless chuck is tightened by turning the chuck itself after the spindle lock has been unlocked; this is usually done by pressing it in.

Bits come in a variety of shapes and sizes suited to different functions and materials. For basic DIY, you will use mainly twist bits (the straight ones with a thread) for drilling holes, but you need the right bit for the material used. A masonry bit is very tough and has a tungsten carbide tip. Wood bits have a sharp cutting thread and point for accurate positioning. Metal bits are made from hard steel and have a v-shaped tip but can also be used for wood.

The size of bit used will depend on the size of hole needed to accommodate the screw. Like screws, bits are sized by number: the smaller the number, the finer the bit. Both twist and masonry bits are sized in millimetres with the most widely used ranging from 2mm to 10mm.

A countersink bit has a short, wide pointed end. It drills shallow cone-shaped recesses in wood for countersinking screws – that is, allowing the screw head to be flush with, or below the surface. Screwdriver bits include flat-tip and cross-head versions.

You can buy a set of drill bits that includes masonry, wood and metal bits as well as countersink and screwdriver attachments. They are inexpensive and usually come in a neat box for safe-keeping. Other attachments for power drills can turn them into a rotary sander, a polisher or a rust remover.

in a fix

Looking for a simple nail or screw in a DIY superstore can be a nightmarish experience as you wander up and down long aisles filled with a huge, confusing variety of sizes, shapes and strange names. Often there are helpful information panels above the merchandise explaining the different types and what they are used for. However, matching the diagrams to the actual products is not always straightforward so if in doubt ask an assistant (or try asking the bloke in dusty clothing and big boots standing next to you – he's probably a builder and may be delighted to recommend the right fixing for the job). Nails are easy to use and only require a suitable hammer and a steady hand to knock them into place, but most jobs are better done using screws which provide stronger grip and more support. Screws are also easy to unscrew if you make a mistake, want to take something down or move it to a different position. When you have found the basics you can then investigate the numerous ingenious fixings from cup hooks to coat hooks, heavy-duty gate hinges to tiny delicate box hinges, and a variety of feet, castors, rings and knobs which will inspire and tempt you into tackling more adventurous tasks.

tacks
Short, tapered nails with a large head and sharp point. Easy to use. Mostly for fixing carpet and fabric where the large head keeps it in place.

panel pins
Thin nails with a small head for when screws are too big and may split the wood, such as fixing panels or boxing in. Go in easily and are barely visible.

nails
Available in a huge variety of shapes and sizes. Unless you are into real building work you will use mostly wire nails which are oval in cross section and have a solid, slim head. A lost-head nail has a head that is not much wider than the nail, is therefore less visible and can be knocked below the surface of the wood with a nail punch.

washers
Disks of rubber, metal or plastic with a hole in the middle. They have a variety of uses including forming a seal in plumbing, preventing a screw head or other fixing from penetrating too far into a material or protecting a surface or component from damage.

screws

More efficient than nails. Screws have a thread which bites into whatever material is being screwed into giving a firm fixing. They come in various types and sizes which are described by length and diameter. This is referred to as the 'gauge' which is given a number from 1 to 20, the highest being the thickest. The most commonly used gauges are 6, 8 and 10. The size depends on the use – thicker and longer for heavy jobs to bear a lot of weight and slimmer ones for thinner materials and lighter jobs. Brass screws are often used for good-quality wood as they look great, however, the metal is weak and overtightening can shear off the screw head.

Screws are fixed by a screwdriver that fits into a slot in the screw head. There are two types – the 'slotted head' with a straight groove across the centre, and the 'cross-head' with a cross-shaped indentation. A flat-tip screwdriver is used for slotted heads. A cross-head screwdriver has a pointed end that fits into the cross-shaped slot which doesn't slip. There are various shapes of screw head but the most common are countersunk which will lie flush with the surface, and round-head which won't.

hollow wall and door fixings

Sometimes called 'toggle' fixings, these enable a screw to be fixed into a hollow wall or door where a normal screw and plug would have nothing to grip or fit into. The fixing is fitted into a pre-drilled hole and when screwed tight the outer casing folds up against the inner face of the wall or panel to keep the screw firmly in place.

wallplugs

For a screw to grip securely into masonry, a plug must first be inserted into the hole. Wallplugs are commonly made of plastic and come in all sizes to suit screws. There are a number of other plugs for use on soft masonry or hollow walls such as plasterboard. Threaded plugs screw directly into the wall. Nailable plugs consist of a nail with a plug attached which is hammered into a pre-drilled hole.

knock-down fittings

Fixings required to assemble flat-pack furniture are normally included. They are made specifically for the product so may look different from standard ones. For tightening bolts you may need an Allen key. This fits snugly into a hexagonal socket in the head of a bolt and is then turned. These are often supplied with the product, but if not a set of several different sizes can be bought quite cheaply.

material world

Keep a supply of ingredients for everyday DIY jobs, general repairs and maintenance.

storecupboard supplies

Keep the following in your storecupboard. Stock small quantities so they don't go off.

abrasive paper

Also called sandpaper, it is invaluable for smoothing sharp edges and rough surfaces. Available in different grades from coarse to very fine. Wet and dry papers are used with water for an extra smooth finish.

general-purpose filler

For filling holes in walls, ceilings and woodwork. Available in powder form – which is made into a paste by adding water – or ready mixed in a plastic tub. Although the ready-mixed type is convenient and the right consistency, it is more expensive and hardens if the lid is not put on properly or it is kept for more than a few months.

wood stopper

For filling holes in woodwork that is to remain unpainted. Comes as a stiff, ready-made paste in a tub or tin and is available in a variety of wood colours.

PVC insulating tape

Wrap round any wires that may be exposed when changing light fittings.

masking tape

Invaluable for tricky paint jobs such as window frames. Can be used on a drill bit to mark the required depth of a hole or as a guide for straight cutting through pipes and wood.

PTFE tape

Fine, thin tape wound round the threads of screwed plumbing joints to make a good seal and prevent leaks. Useful in place of a washer in emergencies.

oil

Fine oil is an easy solution to squeaky doors and acts as a lubricant to facilitate unscrewing old fixings. Available in a spray can, it comes with a long thin tube for aiming accurately into deep crevices.

white spirit

A solvent for oil-based paints is vital for cleaning paintbrushes and splashes. Also useful for preparing old woodwork for re-painting and getting rid of greasy stains.

materials

Finding, choosing and using the right materials is essential for successful DIY.

wood

A pleasing material to work with. It feels and smells good, and is easy to use providing you stick to straight lines. It comes in a variety of lengths, widths and thicknesses. Solid wood (referred to as timber) comes sawn (rough) or planed (smooth). Ignore the rough stuff. Planed is best for interior jobs: it looks nicer and won't give you so many splinters. Narrow lengths of wood (often called battening) are used for construction purposes, for holding something up or fixing something to. Smaller strips can be used for decorative and strengthening purposes such as shelf or door edging. Stronger, chunky sizes are used for frameworks, installing baths or building interior walls. Wider sections are used as skirting boards, pelmets, fascias, shelving and floorboards.

Most wood sold for building work is cheap softwood. It comes from coniferous, sustainable forests, so you don't need to feel guilty about using it. It has an open grain and can be painted, but also looks

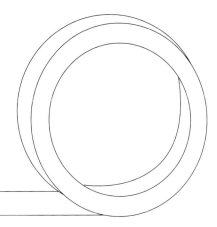

nice varnished, waxed or stained. Hardwoods are much more expensive and have denser, more interesting grains. They are used for worktops, furniture and posh shelving. Veneers are very thin slivers of hardwood glued onto cheaper wood or reconstituted wood, such as chipboard. They have the subtler colours and grains of hardwood without being so expensive, although some of them look a little cheap as the edges have an obvious join and are not very convincing. However, they can be practical and look perfectly okay for shelving and the odd cupboard door.

Manufactured boards are also made from reconstituted wood that has been sliced, ground or chopped up and then glued together again with bonding agents. It comes in various forms including plywood, MDF (medium-density fibreboard), chipboard and blockboard. Plywood and MDF have a smooth finish suitable for painting and are used for panelling and boxing in; MDF can also be used for doors and furniture. Chipboard has a smooth finish but is very porous so is mostly used as a lightweight base for laminated shelving, worktops and flooring. All the boards are available in various thicknesses and sizes.

metal

Beginners will use metal in the form of tubing for shower curtains and wardrobe rails, and perhaps some copper piping for simple plumbing jobs. Stainless steel and zinc sheeting can be used for worktops or splashbacks but is difficult to cut so should be used for straightforward jobs.

plastic

Plumbing fittings such as sink, washing machine and dishwasher wastes are all made from plastic and are very easily assembled with no need for adhesives or heat. Plastic mini-trunking is used for concealing exposed electric wiring and plastic edging strip is used for tiling. Plastic sheeting is sometimes used in place of glass for shower screens, picture frames and other places where glass would be too heavy or constitute a safety hazard. Thicker acrylic sheet is not an easy material for amateurs to deal with so either buy it ready cut and finished or get a professional to do it.

DIY stores are full of plastic mouldings, covings, edging strips, decorative panels and various twiddly bits. Most of these will be shunned by discriminating, style-

conscious shoppers but a few, like plain ceiling covings, can be used effectively.

glass

Glass is wonderful stuff, but can also be quite dangerous. You are strongly advised to buy it ready cut to the exact size required. Glaziers will do this for you; they will also polish the edges so that they are neater and safer. As well as its obvious use in windows, doors and picture frames, glass is frequently used for shelving and shower screens. These will need to be of special toughened safety glass so, once again, get it ready cut and finished.

A wide variety of glass is now available as it is increasingly being used for cool, modern interiors. Wired safety glass is chic as well as sensible and looks very architectural. Etched glass is all the rage; it filters light beautifully as well as providing privacy. Glass bricks (as used in Modernist houses in the 1920s and '30s) are now very popular again and come in several finishes and colours. They are quite easy to use and, with care, can look stunning. Mirror glass is available in ready finished sheets of various sizes with pre-drilled holes for fixing to a wall or door (or even ceiling!).

safety first

The increasing interest in interiors and number of people taking up DIY has led to a corresponding – and alarming – increase in the number of accidents involving home improvers.

Falling off a ladder is easy, as is slicing fingers, severing arteries and burning skin. Taking precautions and following instructions is essential for all fun-loving people who value their health and bodies.

Everyone should have a first-aid kit in their home. Make sure it is fully stocked with the all the essentials before embarking on any form of DIY.

As well as the danger of damage from saws, hammers and drills, other potential hazards to health come from dust, fumes and chemicals. Paint, paint strippers, varnishes, adhesives and fillers are all potentially harmful so it is essential that you follow all instructions and heed all warnings.

labelling

Many products are harmful to the touch as well as giving off potentially dangerous fumes. Even paint fumes can cause dizziness and mild nausea so ensure there is plenty of ventilation; open all the windows in the room you are working in, but keep doors closed to prevent the fumes carrying to other areas.

ALWAYS read the labels on any product BEFORE opening. Look for the following symbols: Harmful, Toxic, Highly Flammable and Corrosive.

Harmful

Toxic

Highly Flammable

Corrosive

gloves

Normal household gloves will protect against germs and possible skin irritants, but wear longer and thicker rubber gloves when using strong chemicals and corrosives. It is a good idea to wear heavy-duty gloves when handling heavy or rough materials with sharp edges, but be careful they don't get in the way and reduce grip or dexterity.

goggles

Eye damage can be caused by flying sawdust or metal particles, sprays and splashes from paints and other potentially harmful liquids, so have a pair of goggles handy. Don't, however, allow them to increase the risk of injury by impeding your vision for tasks where accuracy is important.

face masks

There is already enough pollution around without subjecting your lungs to yet more noxious substances so wear a mask to protect you from dust and fumes but make sure you get the right mask for the job: DUST For cutting and sanding wood and smoothing down filler a simple, inexpensive, fibrous paper mask held on with elastic will suffice. You may look like an extra from Planet of the Apes, but never mind. FUMES Many of the new products involved in painting, varnishing and sealing are quick-drying. This is made possible only with the use of sophisticated solvents, some of which give off harmful fumes. The instructions will recommend the use of a respirator mask which are usually made from moulded rubber, formed to fit snugly round the nose and mouth, with an adjustable strap to keep it tight. A special filter fits into a round breathing area. You may sound like the beast from the deep, and look like a storm trooper from Star Wars, but at least you will be conscious. It is important when buying a masks that you get the correct filter for the chemical involved: the instructions on the product will tell you which one, but if in doubt ask an expert or telephone the manufacturers.

ladders

Always make sure the feet of ladders and stepladders are on a level surface. Set a ladder up so the foot is 1m (3 ft) away from the base of the wall for every 4m (12 ft) of ladder height. If you are scared of heights get someone to stand at the bottom (or persuade them to do the job for you). Make sure that stepladders are fully unfolded and all four feet are on the ground and level. Don't wear flip-flops, backless footwear or high heels when using ladders as you will look silly and probably fall off. Even if you don't, your feet will soon start to hurt so sturdy shoes or boots are best.

clothing

Scarves, necklaces and long floaty clothes are potential death-traps. Carefully disarrayed hair looks sexy but that overlong fringe could cause you to make a fatal error, so tie it back or bundle it into a nice hat. It's sensible to keep your arms and legs covered to guard against cuts, grazes and splashes. Wear comfortable footwear that is flexible and preferably covers the whole foot. Tuck in long laces to prevent them getting caught up in machinery or tripping you up. You don't have to eschew fashion completely – work clothes are cool anyway – but be aware that paint won't wash out and some products can bleach or even burn holes in clothing.

jobs for the girls
an introduction to the core DIY skills

DIY encompasses everything from knocking a nail into a wall to building an extension with an en-suite bathroom. The skills detailed in this chapter will encourage you to use a screw rather than a nail and enable you to put up a natty loo-roll holder and a smart shelf in the en-suite, but not how to build it.

Many a nice home has been turned into an estate agent's nightmare by over-enthusiastic and over-confident people insisting on doing-it-themselves. Home 'improvements' can actually ruin a property and the term 'fitted kitchen' is often plainly untrue. It is a wise DIYer who recognises her own limitations and sets realistic goals. The shape, size and style of your home will dictate how much you can or can't do, as well as what you should or shouldn't do. If you have a beautiful house with vast rooms, high ceilings and wonderful architectural detailing then your DIY activities should be limited to enhancing its inherent characteristics and keeping it in good repair. If you have a small, featureless space then you may want to jolly it up a bit and, if your living quarters are small, you will probably benefit from a few more shelves. A bit of judicious DIY can transform tatty into smart, cramped into cosy and horrible into rather nice.

Drilling your first hole is one of life's milestones: once you have done it you will probably want to do it again. In fact, if you want to put up anything more complex than a single, small hook you will need to drill several holes. Getting those holes in the right place will ensure everything is straight and on the level; doing so will reveal the true meaning of the spirit level. Possession of a power drill will increase your power base and propel you towards bigger and better things. Once you have learned to fix a simple strip of wood to a wall the world of DIY will open up before you.

Even apparently complex jobs such as putting in a new kitchen often involves nothing more than drilling holes and putting in screws. Making the holes and getting them in exactly the right place is not always as easy as it sounds but then again it's not rocket science. With patience, practice and an understanding of the principles of wall construction it is perfectly possible for amateurs to produce professional-looking work.

Mastering these basics skills won't turn you into a craftsman but will enable you to carry out simple jobs that will turn your home into a more convenient, functional and rather more stylish place. Once you have the confidence to tackle the simpler tasks it is often a relatively small step to the more ambitious projects. On the other hand, knowing what is involved in Doing-It-Yourself may be enough to make you decide to stick to the easy stuff – and feel much better about paying someone else do the big jobs.

the hole story

A great many DIY jobs involve fixing things to walls and to do this you will almost certainly have to make some holes. But before drilling into any walls, floors or ceilings it is very important to find out where any electricity cables, gas or water pipes are likely to be and take care to avoid them. The consequences of drilling into any of these could be death and disaster. Don't drill near sockets or immediately above, below and around light switches or light fittings. Various inexpensive, battery-powered devices are available which light up to indicate the presence of metal pipework in walls or under floors. Similar instruments are also available to detect the position of electrical cables.

size matters

Drilled holes are nearly always to accommodate a screw, the most common form of fixing. It is almost impossible to screw directly into plaster, concrete or brick so you will need to use a power drill and masonry bit. The depth and diameter of the hole will depend on the size of the screw and length of the wallplug you are using. A certain amount of dust and debris will collect at the far end of the hole so you need to drill a little deeper than the length of the wallplug. To ensure the hole is the right size, wrap a piece of tape around the drill bit to mark the depth required or use an 'adjustable depth stop' which are sometimes supplied with a power drill.

off the wall

Walls are not necessarily straightforward. If they are made from plaster on brick or blockwork you should be able to drill a hole in them fairly easily with a standard power drill, but if they are made from concrete you will need one with more power. Tools can always be hired so you don't need to spend a vast amount of money on expensive equipment. Soft walls can also be a problem as a small hole can easily turn into a large chasm, so you may need to use threaded wallplugs. These can also be used on hollow partition walls: they can be screwed directly into plasterboard but you will to be careful as a soft or hollow walls may be unsuitable for items that are heavy or structures that are loadbearing.

on the ceiling

Drilling into ceilings can be dodgy and the best advice to novices is not to do it. The certain presence of electric wires and possibly central heating and water pipes, plus the fact that they are not usually solid, makes it a risky business.

Ceilings usually consist of sheets of plasterboard nailed to wooden joists (supporting beams) and then plastered. In older houses the ceiling plaster is applied to thin strips of wood known as lath. The plaster on an old ceiling may be thick enough to accommodate a fairly deep hole and for newer ceilings, a threaded fixing can be used on plasterboard. However, if you want to hang something heavy you will have to find a joist so you have something solid to screw into. Finding one is not always easy but you try tapping along the ceiling until you find an area that doesn't sound hollow. If this area extends right across the ceiling then you can be pretty confident you have found a joist. Some ceilings in flats are solid concrete and, as with concrete walls, are difficult to drill into.

screwed up

Screws can be fixed into most wood quite easily so a deep, pre-drilled hole is unnecessary. However, the screw will go in easily and more accurately if there is a narrow hole to start if off and guide it in; this is called a pilot hole. You can make one using a drill with a fine bit or a bradawl. If you are putting up hooks or fixings that have a screw thread attached they will also be easier to screw in, and will go in straighter, if you drill pilot holes first. Nails don't normally need a hole but if they are very long, or the wood very thick, they will benefit from being helped on their way via a pilot hole. This will also reduce the risk of the nail bending, going in at the wrong angle or splitting the wood.

When a piece of wood is being screwed onto something else – another piece of wood or a wall, for example – it is a good idea to drill a clearance hole for the screw. Drill right through the first piece of wood so that you can use a bradawl to mark the position on the other piece of wood or the wall. If you are screwing into wood and don't want the head of the screw to show, then you will need to countersink the screw. This involves drilling a shallow crater (using a countersink) at the top of the drilled pilot hole so that the screwhead disappears. This crater can then be filled with wood filler to give a smooth surface.

drill call

Making holes in materials other than masonry and wood can be tricky. When drilling into ceramic tiles – putting up a shower attachment or towel rail, for example – care is needed to avoid cracking or chipping. Stick a piece of masking tape on the surface of the tile to help locate the drill bit, stop it slithering and shooting off across the tile. Use a masonry bit but set the drill to rotary action – hammer action will damage the tile – and use a slow speed.

Similarly, when drilling into metal make a small dent with a nail punch, or a bradawl if it is fairly soft, and place the v-shaped end of the metal bit into this dent before starting to drill. If you have to drill plastic-coated laminates always drill downwards through the top of the surface: drilling upwards from below can cause the laminate to crack.

drilling a hole

Check there are no wires or pipes in the wall. Mark where you want the centre of the hole to be. Place the point of the drill bit firmly on this mark at a 90 degree angle to the wall.

Turn on the drill. Keeping it as level and straight as possible, push the drill bit gently into the wall. Continue pushing until the hole is drilled to the depth required.

Insert a wallplug into the drilled hole and tap gently into place with a hammer.

To fix your item (such as a coat hook), place the item against the wall so the screw hole and drilled hole line up, insert the screw, hold firmly in place and begin to tighten using a screwdriver.

on the level

For any job to be done properly, accurate measurements must be made. This involves measuring spaces, lengths, heights, depths, amounts and angles. Marking things is also important, whether it is a small dot for a screw, a straight line for cutting along or more complicated marks on walls for lining up against. Getting things straight, parallel and level is a vital part of getting things to look right and fit together properly. This involves tapes, rules, try squares, swinging plumb lines and delving into the spirit level world.

straight talking

Be warned: walls, floors and ceilings are never 'true'. They are neither perfectly flat nor perfectly straight. Exact right angles rarely exist between walls, floors and ceilings so don't assume the measurements at both ends of a room will be the same. Alcoves are particularly prone to inconsistent measurements so always measure across the back as well as across the gap at the front, and take measurements at intervals all the way down.

When drawing dots or lines to mark the position of fittings and fixings, always use a spirit level to make sure they are parallel and straight. Don't rely on your 'eye' and don't take measurements up from the floor or down from the ceiling for the reasons mentioned above. For long distances use a ruler and a length of wood as a guide, but always in conjunction with a spirit level as wood is never perfectly straight and may have quite a bend in it. A swinging plumb line – which consists of a heavy weight on the end of a long length of string – will automatically create a vertical when allowed to hang free from a nail at the top of a wall and is often used for marking up guide lines for wallpaper. However, this really needs two people – one to hold the plumb line in place and the other to draw the guide lines – so it may be easier to stick to a spirit level and a straight edge. To stop the plumb line swinging, place the weighted end in a bucket of water.

When taking a measurement always keep the tape measure straight and level – even a very slight angle will affect accuracy. To mark up a length of wood for cutting, put a small pencil mark on the edge against the required measurement. If the wood is narrow, use a try square to draw a line right across. For wider pieces, measure along both sides and join up the dots. To ensure accuracy for longer cuts mark the measurement in the middle as well as the edges then join up the three dots.

making your mark

Marking out panels will require extra care to ensure accuracy. Use as many of the finished edges of the material as possible as cutting a perfect right angle is difficult. Mark up the measurements at frequent intervals and use a long straight edge such as a metal ruler to draw the lines. Check right angles with a try square or a set square. Better still, get it cut to size at the DIY store or timber merchants.

When putting up a fitting or a small item, such as a cupboard, where two or more screws are required, it is a good idea to mark and drill just one hole to start with. Once the first hole has been made, put up the item using a single screw and then, using a spirit level, reposition the item and mark the position of the other holes. Remove the first screw and the item before drilling the other holes.

cutting edge

Unless you are very canny, you will not be able to avoid cutting something at some-time. Cutting usually involves a little danger, but with a modest selection of tools and a few good tips, you can cut perfectly straight lines in wood, metal, plastic and other hard stuff, such as tiles, and still have all digits intact. 'Measure twice, cut once' should be your mantra. In the excitement of creativity it is easy to misread a measurement and the resulting mistakes can be costly as well as extremely irritating.

The quality of a cut dictates the quality of the finished job. Just as a bad haircut detracts from a stunning outfit, so a bad DIY cut ruins an otherwise smart interior. While you may consider trimming your friend's fringe, you probably wouldn't attempt a full Nicky Clarke; likewise if a DIY job involves sophisticated cuts get someone else to do it.

wood cuts

Wood is fairly easy to cut with a suitable, sharp saw. In order to achieve a clean, straight cut it is necessary to co-ordinate hand with eye, and have an affinity with the third dimension. As well as controlling the saw so it keeps to a straight line, you must make sure the blade is cutting down at an angle of 90 degrees – if not you will end up with an angled cut that does not look very good and will cause fitting problems.

Short cuts – such as sawing a length from a narrow piece of wood – are not too difficult but a longer cut requires more skill or a specific tool to produce a neat finish. Keeping straight is not easy for beginners but it helps if you have a sharp cutting tool and something to hold the material firmly. There are several workbenches on the market. Although the name may conjure up images of huge structures made from great slabs of wood, the most basic DIY version consists of two lengths of wood on top of a metal frame and the whole thing folds up for easy storage. As well as providing a surface for working, a vice mechanism allows you to clamp a piece of wood or other material between the two lengths of wood to hold it firmly in place for easier cutting, drilling and sanding.

saw points

Make sure anything to be cut is on a level surface and held securely by clamps or a vice (foot). To cut with a handsaw, start by placing the upper part of the saw blade (the bit near the handle) on the marked spot on the edge of the wood. Then dig the blade gently into the wood and draw it backwards a little way to cut a small nick. Using the nick to locate the saw blade – making sure that it is vertical and is lined up with the cutting line – start sawing by pushing the blade forward and pulling it backwards.

To begin with you may find the saw sticks and you have to keep re-starting, but once you get into a regular rhythm try not to stop until you have cut through. Keep an eye on the cutting line to make sure you are maintaining a straight line: you will find that a sprinkling of sawdust obscures it from view and you have to blow it away at frequent intervals. If your cut is deviating wildly from its prescribed path then stop and try straightening up by re-positioning the blade. Ragged cuts can always be tidied up with abrasive paper.

Alternatively, use a power jigsaw. Most modern models will make straight and curved cuts in wood up to approximately 70mm (2¾ inches) thick and metal up to 4mm (¼ inch) thick, as well as most plastics. Variable speed allows you to slow down for tricky bits

A simple butt joint as used for wall battens.

Plain skirting board can be joined using a simple butt joint.

A mitred joint as used on the architrave around a door or a picture frame.

A mitre block for use with narrow strips of wood and beading. 45 degree slots are used to accurately cut mitred joints.

dustblower keeps the cutting line visible; some even extract the dust as you go. Various other features help keep all edges straight. A base plate helps to keep the drill vertical for straight lines and various features are incorporated for cutting curves and bevelled edges.

Circular power saws are bigger than power jigsaws and are only really worth buying or hiring if you are cutting up a lot of panels or are using very thick wood.

cut down to size

Whatever you use, beginners will find that any cut longer than about 150mm (6 in) is likely to produce a less-than-perfect edge. This is okay if it isn't going to show, but for shelves, worktops and panels used for boxing in pipes or doors a neat edge is essential.

A machined edge is best and the bigger the machine the better. Most DIY stores have such machines and will cut wood (straight cuts only) to your exact measurements. The service is either free or carries only a small charge, sometimes the first few cuts are free and then the charge kicks in. Before you go to buy wood find out the dimensions of standard lengths and widths so that you can work out the most economical way of getting the sizes you need. Work out exactly what you need and write down all the measurements with diagrams as well. Load the uncut lengths into your trolley and take them, and the diagrams with all the correct measurements, to the assistant in the cutting service area. Sometimes these services are much in demand and queues build up so don't ask for too much at one time. Try to go at less busy times and telephone first to make sure the cutting service is available.

a word about joints

The simplest way to join two pieces of wood together is with a butt joint, where two edges are butted together and secured with nails, pins, screws or wood glue. This is fine when the joint is to be covered up or painted but for a job such as putting new architrave round a door or beading around a floor edge a mitred joint is necessary for a neater finish. This involves cutting an accurate 45 degree angle which can be constructed using simple maths and a protractor or, for narrow pieces of wood, a mitre block.

cutting remarks

Wherever and whenever possible DIY virgins should stick to straight lines. Negotiating corners, curves, pipes and protuberances can turn simple jobs into lengthy procedures so think hard before trying to fit your way around them.

Cutting out slots for a single pipe or straight-sided object is okay as you can cut a straight-sided slot to accommodate them. However, this is not quite as straightforward as it sounds. Making the two cuts which form either side of the cut-out is simple but it is impossible to cut the third side with a conventional saw as there is never enough room for the blade.

cut it out

If the indent is not very deep you can use a coping saw – a frame saw with a very thin, removable blade – that can be passed through a drilled hole at one corner of the cut and then fixed into position between pins. In theory, you should then be able to cut along the other edge and the blade swivels to allow you to cut out holes and curves. This is not easy, however, and can only be used for thin wood.

Cutting a chunk out of a worktop would not be possible; you would have to use a jigsaw, drilling large holes in the corner to allow the blade to fit through. Slots for slim pipes are more straightforward as you can drill a hole slightly larger than the pipe and then cut in from the edge to meet the hole forming a round ended slot which will, hopefully, fit snugly round the pipe. Beginners often end up with a less than neat fit so unless you are confident you can do a good job don't risk messing up expensive materials.

on edge

It can be difficult to get a neat edge when cutting through laminates as the plastic coating is brittle. To minimise damage always cut with the top surface face up when using a power saw or when using a jigsaw, which cuts on the upstroke, cut with the 'top' surface facing downwards. Alternatively, get the assistant in the DIY store or builder's merchant to cut it for you.

Plastic edging and piping is easy enough to cut but sheeting is more troublesome. Soft plastic can clog saw teeth and thicker, harder materials such as acrylic sheeting will crack unless it is cut carefully. Acrylics are also expensive so get them cut and finished professionally.

hacked off

Cutting metal is easier than it sounds but to begin with it is best to avoid sheet metal or heavy metal fittings or fixings.

Many home improvements involve cutting metal tubing which is used for curtain poles, wardrobe fittings and pipework. A small hacksaw with a thin, replaceable blade is adequate but it can be difficult to control as the blade is also quite flexible.

Placing a piece of tape around the tube as a guide will help you to see if you are cutting at 90 degrees but an easier option is to use a pipe cutter. This is an ingenious device which holds the pipe in place while a small blade, tightened by a hand-turned screw, makes a neat, straight cut. Cutting metal produces a lot of heat so don't touch the edges of the metal or the saw until things have cooled down. Tidy up ragged edges with a file or abrasive paper but be careful not to cut your fingers on any sharp metal.

To cut through thick metal, ceramic or stone it will be necessary to use an angle grinder. This power tool has a tough, circular blade which whizzes round fast enough to cut through very

cutting round a pipe

1. Mark the cutting lines on each side of pipe.

hard materials. They are not expensive and look small and manageable, but the effort needed and the noise and dust generated during their use means they are more suited to builders than beginners.

Special cutters can be bought for making clean straight cuts in ceramic tiles, but for awkward shapes you will need to use a cutting tool and a pair of snips which takes care and a certain amount of skill. Pliers have a cutting blade which will cut through electric cables and wiring and some have a little notch for stripping off the plastic coating for wiring up plugs. Cutting knives can be used for paper, vinyl, carpet and thin plastic. The chunky ones with replaceable blades are versatile as a variety of blades are available including curved ones for cutting carpet, and a small saw blade.

2. Measure the distance from the wall to the front of the pipe and mark on the shelf/worktop.

3. Mark the centre of the hole to be drilled for positioning the drill bit.

4. Drill out hole using a power drill.

5. Cut along the marked lines using a saw.

getting it together

Many DIY jobs involve fixing things to walls, fixing things to other things and joining things together. Most things are fixed by means of screw, nail, bolt, glue or, occasionally, double-sided sticky tape. The method of fixing depends on several factors including function, materials involved, size of components, load-bearing requirements, practicality and aesthetic considerations.

Perhaps the simplest fixing is a nail knocked into a wall and, unsophisticated though this is, it is perfectly okay for hanging small pictures and other light-weight objects. A screw will do the same job but will be stronger as it is fixed more firmly into the wall.

Some fittings such as hooks, loo-roll and soap holders are fixed directly to a wall using screws. Shelves, towel rails, blinds and curtain poles are supported or attached using special fixings, brackets and battens which are screwed on first.

It is essential that the correct type and size of fixing is used, and that they are fixed firmly into the wall, ceiling or window frame. Shelves, cupboards, blinds and curtain poles are often required to support a considerable amount of weight as well

as being subjected to constant pressure and movement.

fixed assets

When buying fittings you will find that screws and wallplugs are often provided; this is useful but check they are suitable for the material they are to be screwed into. To get screws to stay in walls you must provide something for the screw to grip on to. Simple plastic wallplugs are usually sufficient for masonry walls but, as discussed in the section on making holes (see pages 22–23), soft or hollow walls will need special fixings. If you want to fix something heavy to a stud partition wall you will need to locate the solid wood support and screw into that. As with ceilings, finding that support may be a matter of tapping until the hollow sound stops, then trying a screw to see if it digs into something solid.

Other DIY jobs involve covering things up. Permanent panels, as used for boxing in pipes or covering unsightly features, can be made from MDF, plywood or solid wood. They are fixed to a wooden framework using panel pins which are very thin and will be virtually invisible.

Where panels need to be removed for access to plumbing, electricity or gas, you will need to use screws, and if the panel is visible use mirror screws.

Skirting board is often nailed directly to the wall with long masonry nails but it is kinder to the wall, the wood, and possibly your fingers, if you use screws. Architrave is narrower and normally has a moulded profile that makes it unsuitable for screws, therefore it is usually nailed in place using long thin pins.

stick 'em up

Modern adhesives are very efficient and some are strong enough to be used instead of nails or screws. They can be useful for poor quality or hollow walls which may be unsuitable for screws or nails, or in places or situations (an awkward corner or proximity to wiring or pipework for example) where putting in a nail or screw could be difficult or even dangerous. However, positioning must be accurate and it is not easy handling and manoeuvring long lengths of wood coated in quick-drying adhesive. Also, bear in mind that anything stuck down will be difficult to remove without damaging the surface and the item, whereas nails and screws can be removed relatively easily. PVA wood adhesives are used in addition to nails and screws to strengthen wood-working joints.

knocking in nails

Locate a nail by holding it in position and giving it several short taps until it is in far enough to stay put so that you can drive it in with heavier blows without endangering your thumb. For very short nails or tacks where there is no room for fingers, push the nail into a small square of thin card which is easier to hold in position and can be torn away when the nail is firmly located in the wall. Use a nail punch to drive the head of a nail beneath the surface for an invisible fixing.

putting in screws

Screws have a thread which needs to dig into something in order to keep it firmly in place. There is a huge variety of screws available with different threads for different materials. Experts would, quite rightly, refuse to generalise; in a situation where they are supporting a lot of weight, using the wrong screw could be

dangerous. However, it is possible to find straightforward, good quality screws that can be used for most jobs although you may have to ask for help in identifying them.

Screwing into wood is relatively easy. The thread of the screw digs its own made-to-measure hole where it sits nice and tightly. Some screws have sharp points and special threads for screwing directly into the wood but a pilot hole will make putting them in much easier and more accurate. Try to use cross-head screws as the cross-point screwdriver is easier to control. Always keep the screwdriver at 90 degrees to the surface to ensure the screws go in straight.

When putting screws into walls, make sure the screw goes into the wallplug and not to one side. If a screw won't tighten then it may be too short or too thin for the hole, the hole may not be providing a suitable grip for the screw, the material may be too soft or too hard or the wallplug is not large enough.

put-up jobs

1. Cut the length of batten required, hold it in position using a spirit level to ensure it is level and draw a line with a pencil across the top. Mark the position of the ends.

2 and 3. Take down the battening and place on a worksurface. Mark the position of the screws making sure they are evenly spaced. Drill through the battening using a twist drill.

4 and 5. Place the battening against the wall and make an indented mark using a bradawl. Make holes in the wall using a power drill and pop a wallplug into each hole.

6. Fix the battening to the wall using screws which go right through the batten and into the wallplugs.

One of the most useful things to put on a wall is a batten – a strip of wood screwed to the wall to which other items such as hooks, shelves, worktops, cupboards and the like can be fixed. Putting up a batten is a passport to greater things and once you have done it you will feel you have earned a certain amount of DIY credibility.

Battening, as it is also called, is widely available. Although the dimensions vary according to the job, the most commonly used battening is what builders refer to as 'two-by-one', which means 2 inches wide by 1 inch thick (50mm x 25mm). What the batten is to be used for will dictate its length, positioning and how you treat the ends but whatever its size the method of putting it up remains the same.

putting up a batten

1. Cut the battening to the length required. Hold it in position against the wall using a spirit level to ensure it is perfectly horizontal and draw a pencil line on the wall across the top of the battening. Mark the position of the ends.

2. Take down the battening from the wall and place it on a workbench or working surface. Along the centre of the battening mark the position of the screws with a bradawl making sure there is not more than approximately 500mm (20 inches) between each one, and placing the end screws not more than 38mm (1$\frac{1}{2}$ inch) from the edge.

3. Using a twist drill that is slightly thinner than the screws, make holes right through the battening at the marked positions (but make sure you don't drill into the workbench or your best table).

4. Hold the battening firmly in position against the wall along the pencil lines you have drawn. Poke a bradawl through each drilled hole in the battening to make an indented mark on the wall.

5. Take down the battening from the wall again and using a power drill make holes in the wall on these indented markings. Pop a wallplug into each drilled hole in the wall.

6. Fix the battening to the wall using screws that are long enough to go right through the batten and tighten in the wallplugs in position in the wall.

Sort out your music collection by putting up a wall-mounted CD rack.

Make sure you're never caught out again by installing new bathroom fittings, including a loo-roll holder.

Make a coat rack by screwing a row of simple hooks to a batten fixed to the wall.

Keep your bathroom tidy by fixing up a new medicine cabinet, complete with mirror for those essential make up checks.

Avoid those last minute searches for your house or car keys by putting up a hook inside the front door (but make sure it is out of reach from the letter box).

Decorate your walls by hanging up that heavy picture frame or mirror at last.

7. Perfectionists will suggest counter-sinking all the screws into the battening before filling, but modern softwoods are usually soft enough to allow you to screw a little tighter so that the screwhead embeds itself in the wood. You can then put filler over the top of the screwheads to hide the fixings and achieve a smooth finish.

what you can use battening for

Putting up a batten allows a long length of wood to be fixed to the wall using a relatively small number of screws. It provides a strong base and suitable material for attaching fixings such as nails, panel pins, screws and hooks and therefore is used for several jobs around the home.

Shelves and worktops are supported by battening that is fixed to walls. It is also used as a framework for boxing in pipes or putting up wall panelling. Battening can be fixed to a wall for hanging heavy weights such as a wallhanging or a large picture and can also be useful on a hollow wall where the batten can be fixed securely to solid wood studs.

Roman blinds are hung from battening and other types of blinds or shutters are often attached to a batten rather than the wall or ceiling. Wood is easier to screw into than walls so it makes sense to put up a length of wood using a small number of long, strong screws and use this for screwing hooks or fittings into. Lighting and curtain fittings can be concealed behind a wooden pelmet attached to a batten. Some DIY jobs involve putting up a temporary batten as a guide against which to line up tiles or kitchen units.

fix it

common repair jobs for around your home

Keeping your home in good order is the grown-up equivalent of tidying your bedroom, but though the task seems uninviting and rather daunting, as soon as you've done it you wish you'd made the effort sooner. If you own your home it makes good sense to look after it in order to maintain its value and remain a desirable property should you wish to sell. But the best reasons for fixing that loose floorboard or squeaky door is that your home will be a much nicer, and possibly safer, place to live in. Major works such as re-plastering walls and ceilings or laying new floors should definitely be left to the skilled professionals, but repairing holes is a doddle and putting on a new skirting board is not too difficult (but getting the old skirting board off can be tricky).

Floors have a big impact on your home so don't be afraid to rip up your tired and tatty floor coverings. If you are very lucky you could find a beautiful wooden or tiled floor beneath which you can clean and restore. If not, ordinary floorboards can be sanded and sealed for the fashionable bare look. Concrete is cool and can be painted or sealed for the chic, industrial style.

Walls and ceilings cannot be ignored, and will attract unwelcome attention if they are in a bit of a state. However, some judicious DIY can make them melt into the background or stand out boldly, whichever you prefer. Although open plan is all the rage and walls are out of favour, novices are strongly advised to leave walls well alone except for patching them up and decorating. Walls play a very important role supporting ceilings, upper floors, roofs and even whole buildings, so don't even think of removing one – the consequences could be disastrous. If you want to open up your space, get a qualified architect or surveyor to advise on how best to do it.

Removing a door will open up a space and is not difficult, and neither is hanging a new one. Getting a door to fit well may be a little more complicated but is definitely not beyond beginners. Windows are trickier as they form part of the structure of a building, but getting them to open or shut smoothly is straightforward enough. New fixtures such as window and door catches will not only work better, but look good too, just as a dull cupboard or door will be transformed by new handles and knobs.

Fixing and repairing are also part of the essential preparation work for painting and decorating, so once your home is looking good it makes sense to ensure that it is safe and secure. Smoke alarms are inexpensive and can save lives while a variety of locks and bolts are available that are both discreet and easy to fix to doors and windows to make them intruder-proof without making your home look, and feel, like a fortress.

things to know about floors

A scruffy or grubby floor will detract from even the smartest furniture and decor so it is well worth investing time and money in this important area. The choice of flooring will depend on your personal preferences and circumstances, but even on a small budget it is possible to produce a great looking base to complement and enhance your interior.

bare is beautiful
... especially if it is limestone, old waxed boards, polished concrete or brand new solid wood. Ordinary floorboards can look good when sanded, painted, varnished or waxed. Old tiles, flags and even concrete can look distressingly beautiful if cleaned up and sealed.

cold feet
Hard floors, particularly concrete or ceramic tiles, can be cold, especially in winter when they can defy even the best central heating. Necessary ventilation under wooden floors can become an undesirable draught around ankles if the gaps are too wide.

quiet please
Your downstairs neighbours may also be pleased at the return of carpet. Bare floors are noisy, particularly hard materials such as tiles that don't absorb any sound. Tiling an entire ground floor may look stunning but will have the intimate ambience of the local swimming pool.

floors matter
The subtlest colours and the chicest furniture will never look any good if your floor is tatty. Light coloured floors make an interior seem larger and using the same floor finish throughout will make it look bigger still.

warm toes
Carpet is making a comeback and rugs are all the rage, which is good news for those who have been longing to pad around in comfort and wish to use the floor for activities other than walking on. But if you can't live with clutter, underfloor heating to warm bare floors is now easier and cheaper than ever before.

health matters
Natural materials are kinder to our bodies as well as the environment so wherever possible stick to wood, natural fibres and additive-free finishes. Asthma sufferers are often advised to avoid fitted carpets but check that your alternative floor-coverings, laminates and any adhesives are free from potentially harmful chemicals.

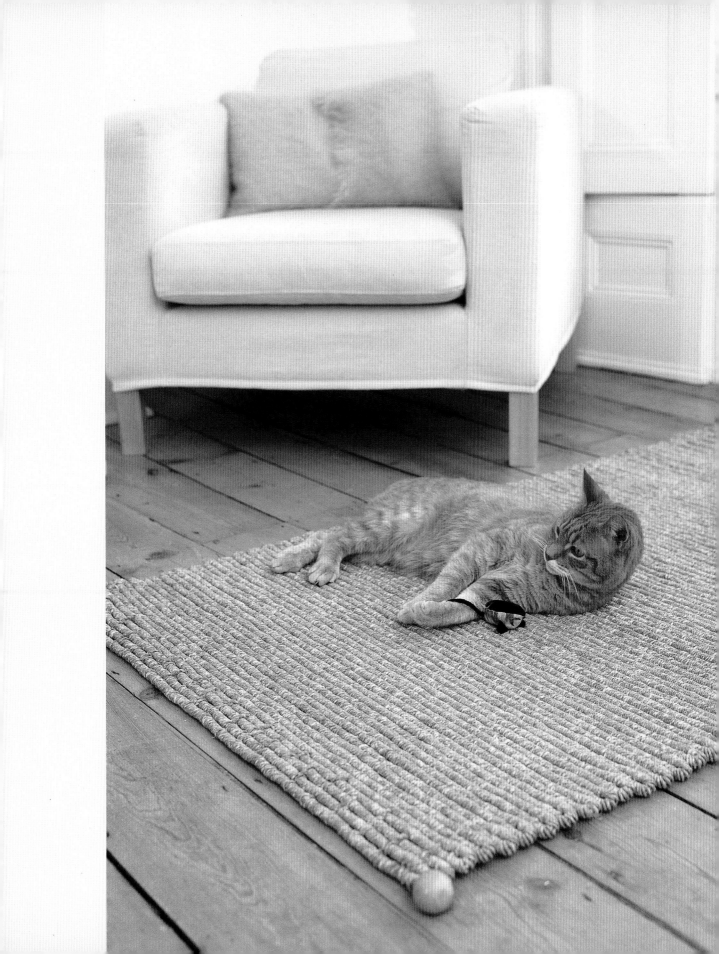

repairing wooden floors

Replacing a floorboard can either be a simple or rather complicated task depending on its length, width and accessibility. If you have a beautiful old floor you may want to get a professional carpenter in who will treat its repair with the care and respect it deserves.

A short length of floorboard in the middle of a room is relatively easy to deal with, but when faced with long boards and edges the job becomes much more difficult. Unless the floorboard is very damaged or unsightly – or is infested with woodworm – it is better to rely on sanding and finishing to make it look okay.

Floorboards come in a variety of widths and thicknesses. Cheap softwood boards, laid as a base rather than a feature, are usually narrow and of a standard width available from timber yards and DIY stores. Old floorboards are often wider so you may have to go to an architectural salvage yard to find a replacement; it may need a little cleaning up before use.

Floorboards are attached to joists, the chunky lengths of wood that form the framework of the floor (and, in upstairs rooms, support the ceiling below). The floorboards run in the opposite direction to the joists and are normally attached with floor nails that have straight sides to minimise splitting and a narrow, one-sided head that sinks into the wood.

replacing a floorboard

Lifting a floorboard should be done with care to avoid damaging those next to it. Ideally you should use a bolster chisel which has a wide flat blade for levering up, and a cold chisel which is strong and long enough to insert under the board to

1. Tap the bolster chisel into the gap near to the end of the board to be removed. Lever gently until the board begins to lift and the nails start to come out.

2. Repeat this process at the other end. Insert the claw of a hammer under the lifted board until there is room to insert the cold chisel.

3. Slide the cold chisel underneath the floorboard towards the next set of nails and repeat the above procedures along the length of the board until it eases out.

4. Fit the new board into position and nail it down to the joist using floorboard nails. Nail at the ends and wherever it crosses a joist.

assist the levering process. Other useful tools include a claw hammer, floorboard saw, nail punch and floorboard nail.

potential pitfalls

If any of the following apply you may want to seek help from a carpenter or simply decide not to bother:

Problem: The floorboard disappears under the skirting: you will have to lift it up in order to pull it out. If it is a long board that is extends under two skirting boards then you will have to cut it in half.

Problem: The floorboard is nailed underneath the skirting: you will have to cut it as close to the skirting board as possible using a floorboard saw.

Problem: The floorboards are tongued and grooved: there is no gap for easy levering.

Problem: The new floorboard sits below the rest of the floor: you will have to put packing underneath (cardboard, hardboard or thin wood will do) where it is nailed to the joists.

Problem: The new floorboard stands above the rest of the floor: you will either have to make the board thinner by planing or cut a recess into the joists to slot the board into.

rejuvenating wooden floors

Bare wooden floors are popular as they give a fresh, modern look to any interior and can be achieved fairly easily and cheaply by sanding and sealing existing floorboards. The condition of the boards will dictate just how easy this is going to be, but as long as they are sound, the surface isn't too uneven and there aren't too many holes it shouldn't be too much of a problem.

Sanding does create a lot of dust and noise, however, so warn your neighbours. If you already have polished floorboards in good condition but feel they are a bit dull or dark, think hard before doing any drastic sanding. Cleaning and re-waxing will lighten them and restore them to a glory you didn't know they had. Solid wood parquet floors should be left to the experts; don't risk spoiling them with inappropriate or poorly executed treatments.

on board

If your home is new or recently converted you may find the boards beneath the floor-covering have been left in their original, unfinished state. Often they are covered with paint splashes and bits of plaster; if these can't be removed easily by scrub-bing and a little paint stripper you will need to sand them. Old floorboards that are very dirty or are buried beneath many layers of paint or varnish will need a thorough sanding to achieve an even finish.

Badly damaged boards should be replaced. Whether you do this yourself depends on the number of boards involved, their position and size (see panel on replacing a board, pages 38–9). Big gaps between the boards are an aesthetic issue as much as anything, although draughts could also be a problem. If all the gaps are very wide then either cover them up again or have the floor professionally re-laid.

unwelcome guests

If you find evidence of woodworm in your floorboards you must check whether it is live. Fresh holes and piles of fine sawdust are indicators that the woodworm are alive and active in which case the floorboards and the joists should be sprayed. Get a reputable company to do this unpleasant job for you; they will provide a guarantee that is valid for several years, which you will need as proof of treatment for any future buyers of your property.

sanding a wooden floor

Secure any obviously loose floorboards and use a nail punch to knock nail heads below the surface; any protruding nails will damage the sanding belt. Remove all furnishings, curtains, etc. and open all the windows. Seal gaps around the door with tape and wedge newspaper at the bottom. Hanging a wet sheet on the outside of the door will also help prevent the dust escaping.

You will need to hire an industrial drum sander for the main floor area and an edge sander for the sides and corners. The hire shop will give you full operating instructions, including how to change the sanding belt.

It is as well to know that a sander won't necessarily behave as you would expect it to. It will make its own way across the floor without much assistance and must be held back to ensure progress is slow and steady. Don't let go or it will run away. Hold the drum off the floor when you switch it on and lower it gently to begin sanding. Once switched on, it is essential to keep moving: allowing the sander to stay in one spot for any length of time will result

1. Using a coarse grain abrasive paper, sand the floor diagonally.

2. Change to a medium grade paper and sand across the boards.

3. Using a fine grade paper, sand up and down until the surface is smooth.

in a smooth, but unwanted, hollow in the floor.

You will need to wear a mask, goggles and ear protection when sanding as the noise of the sander and the dust from old paint and varnish can be hazardous. Several sandings will be necessary, starting with coarse sandpaper to level the floorboards. For this first sanding, move diagonally across the room tilting the machine to change direction and overlapping each run to ensure the whole surface is covered. When you have covered the whole floor switch off, sweep up the dust and then start again, this time sanding diagonally in the other direction. When the floor is flat, change to medium grade sandpaper and continue sanding parallel to the boards. Finally, finish with fine grade sandpaper for a smooth, scratch-free surface. After each stage, repeat the process around the sides and in corners using the edge sander. Use a scraper, a flexible disc sander or wire wool to get right up to the skirting boards and into the corners. When you have finished, vacuum the floor then wipe over the floorboards with a cloth dampened with white spirit ready for finishing.

finishing a wooden floor

Take care not to stain or dirty your newly stripped floor. Unfinished wood is porous and absorbs dirt and spills making it difficult to clean. If you need to walk on it, wear clean socks rather than bare feet (as sweat contains substances best kept off absorbent wood) and don't wait too long before applying sealer.

Sealing involves reducing the porosity of the surface and/or the creation of a coating that will prevent the penetration of dirt while providing a cleanable surface. What you use depends on the look you want plus practical considerations such as use and amount of wear. There is the usual bewildering array of products on the market, with new, improved versions appearing all the time. Sealants roughly divide into varnishes (which form a hard protective coating) and oils (which soak into the wood and are often finished with an application of wax). Varnish can be applied directly onto new or newly finished wood and, depending on the product, will need two or more coats to form a hard, durable surface. Choose between a shiny or matt finish. Sanding by hand between coats will give a better result.

Finishing oils soak into wood and plump up the fibres. Modern versions have additives to help form a waterproof and more dirt-proof surface. Waxing on top of these will produce a soft, mellow finish that will, with diligent application, mature well.

For less than perfect wood, a darker finish will disguise a multitude of sins. Avoid using wood stains as it can be difficult to achieve an even finish, instead use a coloured wood varnish. Most of these varnishes are available in different wood finishes and using a dark colour will achieve a similar effect to a wood stain with less hassle.

If your floorboards are just not good enough to be seen in their natural state, you can always paint them. For a fresh modern look, choose white or grey gloss or floor paint. Applying a wood primer and undercoat first will ensure a smooth, dense finish. A softer effect can be achieved by painting the floor with water-based emulsion paint and adding a dirt-proof coating of clear varnish.

other floor surfaces

Wooden floorboards may be popular but they are not always desirable or practical. Many people prefer the warmth and look of carpet to bare boards. It is often cheaper and easier to carpet a room than fiddle with sanders and sealers.

You will be offered a professional laying service when buying carpet, although it seems expensive it is worth the money. Carpet is heavy and comes in generous widths making it difficult to handle. Fitting it round features and getting it neatly into corners is not easy. A badly fitted carpet will never look good, but if finances are tight and you are desperate to cheer up a small room then do have a go. If doing-it-yourself, avoid expensive thick carpet and opt for thinner foam-backed carpet.

In modern properties chipboard is often used in place of floorboards as it is intended to be covered. Although lacking the character of floorboards, chipboard is draught-free and perfectly flat. The joins are usually invisible so if you want the bare floor look this is a good surface for painting or even sealing with varnish if their colour and finish is even.

Older properties, especially those in the country, sometimes have stone floors.

Stone or slate flags are full of character and add a sense of history, but they can also look stunning when used as part of a pared down, modern interior. Damaged or pitted surfaces are part of the character (call them 'distressed' and you will see them in a different way) so don't be put off by any gaps or discolouring. Scrape off any old blobs of dirt or paint and give the floor a good scrub using soap and water or, if it is very bad, a special stone cleaner (available from your DIY store, builders merchant or floor specialist). Fill any gaps using cement-based exterior filler; this is available in handy sized amounts. Just add water, but don't make it too sloppy. It stays workable for about 20 minutes so work it into the gaps, smooth the surface and wipe excess from surrounding areas. Finish with an appropriate sealer which will soak into the stone preventing dirt penetration. For advice try calling your local stone floor specialist: they love their subject and will usually be happy to dispense helpful information and suggestions for treatments, products and so on.

Tiled floors are often found in older properties. Some are decorative, such as the encaustic tiles used in the halls of Victorian and Edwardian houses, while others are plainer and more prosaic, like the quarry tiles are found in kitchens and less grand homes. Again, if their condition is not great they may respond to a good clean, re-grouting and sealing (see section on tiles, pages 84–5). Missing tiles can be replaced; you may find a match in an architectural salvage yard. The small spaces left by incomplete or missing mosaic tiles can be filled and, if you are feeling clever, painted to match.

Consider freshening up a modern ceramic tiled floor by re-grouting, perhaps with a new colour. Damaged tiles can be removed so that a new one can be fitted into the space (taking care that no sharp bits fly into your eye).

Of course you may just have a boring old concrete floor, but if you are keen on the brutal industrial look you can patch it up and either paint it or just seal it. Clean out holes and cracks removing any loose material then get rid of all the dust (a vacuum cleaner will do this efficiently). Fill the gaps using cement-based exterior filler as above. Concrete is dusty, so you will have to seal it if it is to be left uncovered.

laying laminate

Laminated flooring comes in a range of lengths, widths, materials and prices. Planks or sections fit together with a tongue and groove joint to form a seam-free surface. New systems do not require adhesive. Laminated floors can be laid on top of boards, concrete or any level surface and are usually bought in kits that include spacers (to ensure an even expansion gap) and a tamping block (for tapping joints together without damaging the grooves).

Cover the entire floor with underlay, joining the strips together with adhesive tape. If the subfloor is made of concrete, lay down a thick sheet of plastic to prevent moisture rising up through the underlay.

Place the grooved side of a strip along the longest wall. Put spacers in between to create an expansion gap. Insert the grooved side of a second strip into the first. Repeat until you are close to the wall. Cut the last strip to fit allowing for an expansion gap.

Cut lengths of quadrant beading to fit around room to cover the expansion gap. Use a mitre block to cut the angled joints for the corners (see page 27). Nail the quadrant beading in place with panel pins.

laying carpet

The easiest method is to place carpet grippers – wooden or metal strips with fierce metal spikes – round the edges of the room about 5mm ($\frac{1}{4}$ inch) from the skirting board, spikes facing towards the wall. Fix with short nails or, if the floor is solid, strong adhesive. Cut short strips to fit round alcoves and doorways. Cut the underlay to fit inside these strips.

Put the finished edge of the carpet along one wall making sure it butts right up to the edge. Push the carpet onto the spikes. Next, stretch the carpet across the room and fix it temporarily onto the gripper strip along the opposite wall. Work from the centre towards the corners, pushing and stretching the carpet fixing it onto the spikes. Cut out triangles from the excess at the corners so the carpet can lay flat, then carefully cut along the edges using a knife with a good sharp blade. A long piece of wood or a metal straightedge helps push the carpet towards the wall and acts as a cutting edge. You will be exhausted and bad-tempered by now and vow to pay a professional in future, but hopefully, it will be perfectly okay and any bad bits will be hidden by furniture anyway.

things to know about windows and doors

Repairing, painting and generally making doors and windows in good order not only makes your property look better but is also an opportunity to ensure that they are well-fitting and secure.

they set the style

Different architectural styles have different styles of windows and doors which have been designed to suit the character and proportion of the building. Beautiful windows enhance any property from the inside as well as out. If your windows are not architecturally significant, keeping them painted and in good repair will add to their appeal or detract from their bad points.

they spoil the effect

The wrong windows and doors can ruin an otherwise attractive building. Inappropriate window styles that show a lack of consideration for the history, proportion, materials and construction of a property will not only be aesthetically displeasing but can be financially disadvantageous, often lowering the value of a property quite considerably.

they set the temperature

Open doors and windows let in warm summer sunshine and cooling breezes. Air circulation is necessary for a fresher, healthier environment for you and your building but winter draughts will lower the temperature and increase the heating bills.

they keep things in

Including heat, the cat and your privacy. Well-fitting windows and doors will prevent valuable warmth from escaping and welcome sunshine in. Behind closed doors (and discreetly covered windows) you can create a complete world of your own, known only to you and your loved ones, where you can live a life suited to your own personality, passions and predilections.

they keep things out

Including draughts, the weather, burglars and other unwanted visitors. Solid doors and sturdy windows keep rain and wind in its place. Locked windows and doors will keep precious possessions safe and your insurance company happy.

repairing windows and doors

Doors and windows will be greatly enhanced if they open and shut properly.

doors

Squeaky doors may add atmosphere in a horror film but they are irritating on a daily basis. A squirt of oil on the hinges will solve the problem. Use the spray can variety and put the little tube over the nozzle so that you can aim it accurately into the hinge. If this doesn't work, or only works for a short while, it may be that the door is not hanging properly.

Whether you tackle problems such as a sticking door, or one that doesn't shut, depends on the door, the frame, the hinges and your physical strength. Solid wood doors are very heavy and not easy to handle on your own, so unless you have a strong friend to help you should probably call in a builder or DIY expert. Door frames are not always square, and distortions can be the result of age, central heating, poor quality wood or just that they were badly fitted in the first place.

In order to get a door to fit properly into a frame it is often necessary to remove wood from the edges and this involves using a plane – a tool with a sharp blade for shaving off thin strips of wood, so you will have to buy or borrow one. They are quite efficient and not too difficult to use (make sure the blade is sharp) but it is easy to get carried away and find you have shaved off too much.

If the door rattles and doesn't close properly it could be that the latch is not fit-ting into the latch keep. If it doesn't click into place when closed it could be that the latch is not reaching the keep in which case you should take off the keep and pack it out with some card or wood filler, remembering you may need slightly longer screws when you put it back. Alternatively, the keep may be too near and the latch doesn't have room to spring into the cavity, in which case remove the keep and chisel out a little more wood from the recess before screwing it back into place.

It is not always necessary to take a door off in order to get it to fit better. Look at the hinges and check that the screws are all present and tight, that the hinge fits flush with the frame and that the hinges are positioned so that the door hangs at 90 degrees. Sometimes the screws work loose and tightening them, or replacing them with slightly longer ones, will pull the door back into position. If it still won't shut, find the place where it is not fitting into the frame and either sand it down (if it is a small discrepancy) or plane off the excess (you may have to take the door off to do this). ALWAYS make adjustments to the door, NOT the frame.

door hinges

Hinges come in several forms. The simplest is the butt hinge with two flat rectangular flaps either side of the knuckle. One is screwed to the inside of the doorframe and the other to the edge of the door. They are set into a recess cut to the size and depth of the hinge flap so that they are flush with the woodwork. Just undo the screws on the frame if you need to remove the door. The rising butt hinge comes in two sections, one has a spindle and goes on the frame, the other has a socket which fits over the spindle. The door lifts when opened and so will rise above carpet then close on its own; the door can be lifted off without the need to undo screws (this can be difficult if they have been painted over). They come in left and right-handed opening versions.

Worn hinges cause doors to drop and therefore stick. Fitting new hinges of the same size into the existing recess is easy, but use new, slightly larger screws to ensure they fit tightly into the old holes.

fitting a new door

Doors come in standard sizes and if these fit in your existing frame you may wish to attempt hanging a new one, though it will involve a bit of carpentry. However, if the standard size doesn't fit, or the door is very heavy, then leave it to an expert carpenter.

First, find a friend – you will need someone to help hold the door in position – and you will need two 100mm (4 inch) butt hinges. Make sure the door fits into the frame – there should be a gap of 2mm ($^1/_{16}$ inch) at the top and sides and minimum of 6mm ($^1/_4$ inch) at the bottom (more if you have thick carpet). To check this stand the door in the frame with wedges underneath that raise the door to the correct height above the floor.

Make any necessary adjustments to the door edges using a plane.

With the door in the correct place, mark the position of the hinges 180mm (7 inches) from the top and 250mm (10 inches) from the bottom on both the door and the frame.

Take the door down, stand it on its edge with the hinge side uppermost. Place the flap of the opened hinge against the marks making sure that the knuckle projects beyond the edge (and the hinges are the right way round!). Draw round the flap with a pencil and mark the depth along on the edge.

Now comes the carpentry. With a chisel, make several cuts (the depth of the hinge) across the marked area, taking care not to cut across the pencil line, and also make cuts around the edge. You should then be able to pare away the wood to form a recess the exact dimensions of the hinge flap. Tidy up any rough bits with the chisel. Repeat for the other hinge.

Put the hinge flap in place, mark and drill pilot holes for the screws. Screw into place. Wedge the door in an open position with the unscrewed flaps against the marks on the doorframe. Making sure the knuckle is parallel to the frame, mark round the flap and repeat the carpentry.

Hang the door using one screw in each hinge and check the door opens and closes smoothly. You may need to make the recesses a little deeper, or pack them out with thin card. Now it is okay put in the other screws.

fitting a door

If you have standard sized doorways fitting a new door is not difficult and often easier than repairing an old one.

The simple butt hinge (left) is fine for most doors but a rising butt hinge (right) lifts the door as it opens to fit over carpet.

With the door in an open position place wedges underneath to hold it at the correct height, use the hinges to mark their position on the door frame and the edge of the door.

Draw round hinge. Use a hammer and chisel to cut around the edge and make horizontal slots the same depth as the hinge across the marked area. Pare away the sections of wood.

Neaten up the finished cut out section, hold the hinge in place and mark the position of the screws. Drill pilot holes and screw the hinge to the door.

fixing windows

Dealing with windows is not always an open and shut case.

windows

There are lots of types of windows, some wonderful and some not. They open in a variety of ways. Sash windows go up and down by means of a cord in the side of the frame. Casement windows are hinged vertically to open like a door. Pivot windows have a hinge that allows them to rotate.

Most domestic window frames are made from wood but metal is not uncommon. Many new frames are made from coated aluminium whilst others combine wood and metal in quite complex units. Their construction is surprisingly complicated so don't even think about taking one out or putting in a new one. They are designed to be virtually maintenance-free so shouldn't require much fixing; if they do it is best to call in a window specialist.

Broken or cracked windows are dangerous and insecure as well as looking unkempt and unloved. Get a glazier to replace any glass. A professional will measure the replacement correctly, get it cut, take out the broken bits, fit the new piece, fix it in place and take all the broken glass away. Well worth the money. Glass is rather frightening and dangerous stuff to handle and with new metal window frames the glass is set into the frame and requires special fitting anyway.

Windows that open and close easily are a joy. If they don't it is often over-enthusiastic use of paint either inside or out that prevents them doing so. If the paint is relatively thin you can carefully cut along the join with a sharp bladed knife and use a scraper to open up the gap. If the paint is thick and has seeped through all the joins you will have to resort to liquid paint stripper or a heat stripping gun.

If you can't shut the window properly check where the window fits against the frame – especially the edge where the hinges are as drips of paint or blobs of dirt may be preventing a good seal. Hinges may also stiffen as a result of over-painting, a small amount of paint stripper may help get things moving. A squirt of oil will also loosen up clogged hinges.

Broken sash cords will not prevent you opening a sash window but won't hold the window open. Replacing them involves taking the window out of the frame so get an experienced DIYer to do it. Watch how it is done then tackle the next one.

Old window catches and handles are often coated with layers of paint which makes them stiff and less efficient. If the window frames are wood putting on shiny new ones is relatively simple but the window furniture on old metal window frames is often part of the frame so you will need to rely on paint stripper to free them up.

draughtproofing

Draughts have a knack of finding their way through even the tightest fitting doors and windows, but a wide variety of draught-proofing solutions are available to keep them in check. Some may not be suitable for metal door frames as they are not easy to screw into. The easiest and cheapest form of draught excluder is a flexible foam strip with a peel-off backing which is stuck to the frame where it meets the door or window. It works well but becomes grubby quickly and will need replacing regularly.

A wide variety of excluders are available for doors. Many of them take the form of wood, metal, rubber, plastic or bristles attached to a strip (usually aluminium) which is screwed to the doorframe. Threshold excluders are screwed along the bottom of the door on the inside or outside depending on their construction and that of the door and frame. Among them are weather trims (screwed to the outside of the door and angled to shed water) and brush seals (a row of dense stiff bristles attached to a metal or wooden trim and screwed on the inside of the door). Other ingenious and sophisticated systems are best studied in the DIY store where explanations of how they work and are fixed may be supplied by helpful assistants.

Letterboxes can be very draughty. Fitting an internal flap will help. Some include brush seals but these can be quite fierce and sometimes tear your mail – and your nails.

Draughtproofing for windows is much the same as for doors and varies according to the window type and construction. If any solution seems too pricey, too fiddly or will spoil the look of a window or door you could consider keeping out draughts with heavy curtains or blinds.

An otherwise plain door can be transformed into a design feature by the addition of smart new door furniture. Designs have improved so much in the last few years that it is now possible to buy sleek, modern door handles at very realistic prices as well as countless styles to suit the character of your home.

Before buying, make sure you have the correct fitting for your door. The mechanism is either fitted into a hole in the edge of the door, or is contained in a casing which is fitted on to the surface of the door with a latch keep screwed onto the outside edge of the door frame.

Fitting new knobs and handles on cupboards and chests of drawers can give them a new lease of life. Simple pull handles are very easy as they are just screwed on – but make sure you position them correctly, crooked or uneven spacing will spoil the effect so get out the tape measure and spirit level.

things to know about walls and ceilings

The state of our walls and ceilings is important structurally as well as decoratively. You may wish to draw attention to them with bold colours and patterns or make them dissolve into the background with pale colourings or remove them altogether. Either way they cannot be ignored and will benefit from care and attention.

what they are made of

Solid walls are made of stone, brick, concrete block or solid concrete. Outside walls are usually thicker than internal ones. Inside, walls are normally covered with plaster, a coarse undercoat over which a smooth, dense topcoat is applied.

Uneven surfaces such as stone walls in old properties have a coarser rendered finish. Such properties may have inside walls made from lath – narrow strips of wood nailed to a framework and covered with lime-based plaster – which, depending on the condition of the building, is hard and strong or weak and crumbly.

A cavity wall is a double external wall with a gap in between which may be filled with insulation material.

Plasterboard and plywood can be fixed to solid walls for a smooth surface. A stud partition wall consists of a wooden framework with sheet material, usually plasterboard, nailed to it. Plasterboard is often skimmed with a thin layer of plaster to give a smooth finish and cover up any joins.

they are never 'true'

As discussed in measuring, walls and ceilings are rarely perfectly straight or their surfaces completely smooth. For this reason they don't always join neatly to skirting boards, door and window frames, or each other.

Very uneven, undulating surfaces are part of the 'character' of an old property but in newer buildings it could be a sign of something wrong so get it looked at.

what they do

Structural walls have an important role supporting and strengthening a building. If you want to remove a wall you need to replace it with something else, usually an RSJ (Rolled Steel Joist) which must be specified by a qualified structural engineer or architect. Definitely one for the builder!

Partition walls divide up space so it is possible to take them away without the building falling down. Only an expert will know which are non-supporting walls so DON'T do it yourself!

they can be thin

The sound-proofing efficiency of walls depends on their construction. Party walls which divide one property from another are often built of brick, stone or concrete and are dense enough to provide adequate insulation against the noise from normal daily lives. Internal partition walls, which are often a cavity construction, are not as effective at keeping sound in or out. Flats in converted properties don't always have properly constructed party walls and floors which can cause a problem. Foam, polystyrene or purpose-made insulation boarding can be incorporated into the wall construction.

Minimalism may look chic but hard surfaces reflect sound creating a echoey and unfriendly ambience. Wooden panelling and wall-coverings provide a gentler, warmer environment. Carpets, curtains, soft furniture and books also absorb noise.

fixing walls and ceilings

Cracks on wall and ceiling surfaces are common. They can be caused by a variety of the reasons from very minor to rather worrying. Fine cracks in plaster are often the result of shrinkage due to drying, heat, etc. or vibration from impact such as knocking in nails or drilling a hole.

Bigger cracks appear through settlement due to minor building work in adjacent rooms or properties, or the effects of unusually extreme temperatures. Large cracks or cracks that keep getting bigger can indicate structural faults, so get someone to have a look.

surface tension

Holes in walls can be dealt with quite easily but holes in ceilings are trickier. Working on walls is easier as they are vertical and you have gravity on your side. Ceilings are, and give you, a pain in the neck. One false move and it could end up on the floor. Large holes in ceilings are a job for the experts.

Small to medium sized cracks, holes and dents can be filled using an all-purpose filler. This comes as a powder to which you add water but a ready-mixed version in an airtight plastic tub (which is exactly the right consistency and very convenient, but much more expensive) is also available. Apply using a filling knife or flat scraper. The mixture shrinks slightly when it dries so leave the filling slightly raised from the surface.

When it is dry it use sandpaper to smooth out the bumps. If there is a lot of filler to remove use a coarse paper first and finish with fine. Wrapping the sandpaper round a piece of wood or sanding block will give a more even finish.

holed up

Old screw holes are deep so poke damp newspaper into the hole before applying the filler. For bigger, deeper holes use bonding (a lightweight coarse plaster mix which, when mixed with water, forms a nice thick, easy to handle mixture). When it is dry, rub it down with a coarse sandpaper before applying a top layer of smooth filler.

Repairing really big holes normally involves a bit of re-plastering. This is a skill acquired through years of practice and if you value your property, and your sanity, you will call in an expert plasterer.

filled in

Getting filler into the gaps around frames, skirting boards and the joins between walls and ceilings, can be fiddly and messy, so use a ready-mixed flexible acrylic filler. It comes in a tube with a pointed nozzle which fits into an applicator gun allowing you to shoot accurately into crevices.

fun and fancy

Decorative cornices, mouldings and ceiling roses are often damaged or have lost their definition through layers of paint. If your home is an architectural gem leave any repairs to the expert as the value of your property could be seriously affected by poor and insensitive workmanship. However, in the Victorian and Edwardian era even quite modest homes had mouldings that were mass produced.

If you have the patience you can restore cornices to their former glory by picking out all the old paint. Fortunately, ceilings are usually painted with water-based paint that can be removed by soaking. Wet a small area using a plant spray or sponge to see how easily it will come off. Use various sizes of screw-

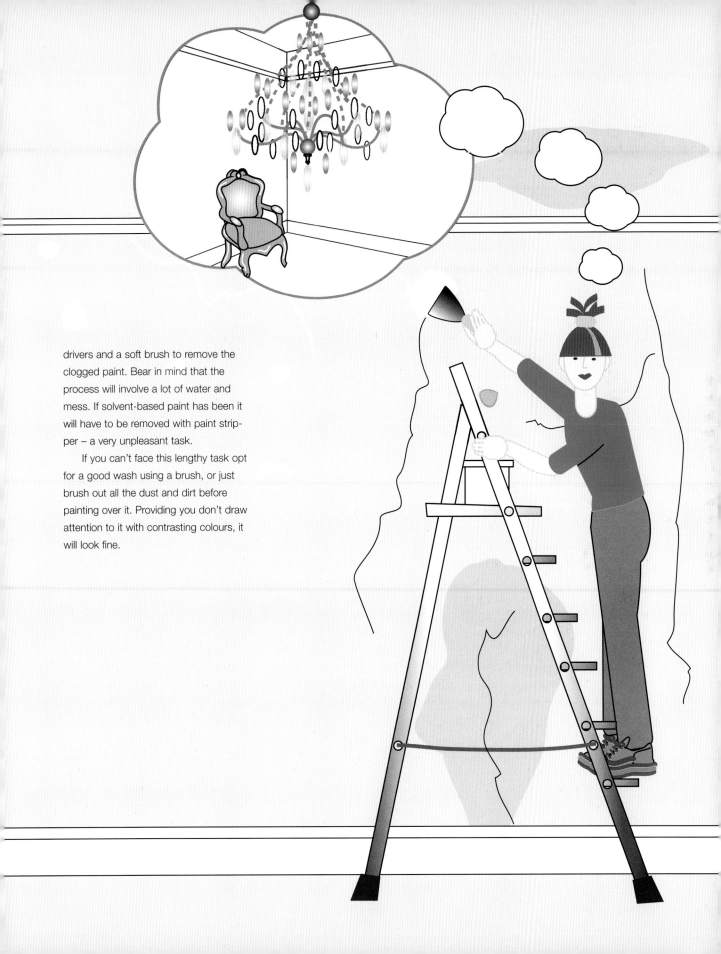

drivers and a soft brush to remove the clogged paint. Bear in mind that the process will involve a lot of water and mess. If solvent-based paint has been it will have to be removed with paint stripper – a very unpleasant task.

If you can't face this lengthy task opt for a good wash using a brush, or just brush out all the dust and dirt before painting over it. Providing you don't draw attention to it with contrasting colours, it will look fine.

safe as houses

It is wise to be security conscious but there is no need to be paranoid. Some home insurance companies insist on a certain level of security before providing cover. Find out before embarking on any security improvements as certain locks and fittings may be specified.

While it is nice to feel no-one can get in, remember once inside with all bolts and locks secured you will not be able to get out easily. Having to fiddle with keys in a fire could be fatal, and if you are taken ill valuable time could be wasted getting to you. Make sure keys are kept in an accessible place (but not handy for burglars), leave a spare set with someone reliable (not often out or away) and give details to close friends and family.

door locks, bolts and spyholes

The two types of locks most frequently used are the deadlocking cylinder rim and the mortice. The cylinder rim lock is used mainly on front doors. A small knob or handle on the inside turns a spring lock to open the door. When the door closes it automatically springs back into place and can only be opened from the outside using a key. An extra turn with the key from the outside will lock it into

position (deadlock) so that it cannot be opened from the inside.

The mechanism of a mortice lock is fitted into a hole in the edge of the doorframe and must be locked and unlocked with a key, although some can be opened and from the inside with a knob or handle.

Fitting cylinder rim locks is not too difficult but they are quite sophisticated mechanisms so it is usual to ask a locksmith. He will make sure everything lines up, works properly and conforms to requirements for insurance.

Fitting a mortice lock involves cutting a deep slot in the edge of the door – drill a row of holes to the required depth and then gouge out the rest with a chisel – in which to fit the 'lock body' and then a shallower slot in the doorframe for the bolt or latch. Now drill a hole into the door to give access to the keyhole – a locksmith will do this accurately.

Replacing a lock is easy providing you get one of similar size and make to fit into the existing holes. Take the old lock to a locksmith or DIY store to make sure. Remember, if your keys have been lost or stolen you only need to replace the internal mechanism – a locksmith will supply a new one complete with new keys.

Hinge bolts screw into the edge of the door – near the hinges for strength – and fit into a recess in the doorframe when the door is closed. Drill a shallow hole in the door for screwing the bolt into, and another in the frame opposite. Chisel out a recess for the locking plate.

Bolts add extra security but as they can only be operated from inside you will be locking yourself in. Make sure you can open them quickly in case of emergency.

Rack bolts fit into the edge of the door and are operated by a key. You will have to drill three holes, one for the barrel, one for the key and one in the frame for the bolt to fit into. Take care to drill straight into the door and the frame – veering off at angle could damage the door and the bolt won't fit properly. Mark the position of the keyhole using a try square.

Spyholes are useful for checking out a visitor before choosing whether or not to open the door. They are simple to install and can be adjusted to fit any thickness of door. Drill a hole right through the centre of the door at eye level. Insert the barrel of the viewer from the outside and screw in the eyepiece from the inside.

A security chain is another wise precaution. The fixed end of the chain is screwed to the doorframe and the loose end fits into a fixing plate screwed to the door. For convenience, position it just below the lock.

window locks

Window locks are a good idea and often required for insurance purposes. There are a number of different styles to suit different styles of window. They work on the principle of locking the window to the frame (or for sash windows, locking the windows together) either with a screw or bolt. They are usually operated with a key which is removed after locking. Some can be locked manually but must be opened with a key. Many use a standard key which is widely available (and therefore can be bought by burglars) but others have keys cut in several hundred variations.

Newer windows are supplied with integral locks and lockable stays, but to secure more traditional, wooden windows it is easy to screw on locks; others will need holes drilling for the bolts and the key. Patio doors are especially the doors so make sure they are fitted with the correct type of lock and fit them top and bottom to prevent them being lifted out of the frame.

security lights and alarms

An outside light operated from inside illuminates visitors and indicates the house is occupied. A security light that comes on when approached will illuminate dark doorways, deter intruders and enable you to find the keyhole in the dark. Though relatively inexpensive and easy to install, outdoor lighting involves drilling through outside walls and taking electricity outside where it needs special insulation to cope with wet weather. This is, therefore, a job for the expert or the experienced.

Alarm and surveillance systems should always be installed by a reputable company as the systems are sophisticated and complicated to set up. Installation will affect your home insurance policy which may impose stringent regulations. There are several DIY versions on the market but you will need expert advice on how to set it up and approval from your insurance company on the equipment and its siting so, once again, leave it to the experts.

Connecting a light or a radio to an automatic time-switch will give the impression that your home is occupied. They can be set to switch on and off several times during the day. However, the regularity of the timing may tip off a

watchful burglar so use it for short periods of absence, or alternatively invest in a more sophisticated switch that will change the timings throughout the week or can be set to random switching.

smoke alarms

Fire can be devastating to property and life so every home needs a smoke detector which gives off a piercing wail when in contact with smoke. There are two main types. Photoelectric devices detect large quantities of smoke produced by slow-burning fires. Ionization devices are more sensitive to small particles of smoke as produced by hot blazing fires. Fortunately, detectors are available that combine both systems and as the incidence of both types of fire can never be discounted it would be wise to opt for one of these.

Battery operated detectors are easy to put up. Don't put them in kitchens or bathrooms where steam can set them off, and don't place them near sources of heat. Hallways and landings are good places. Put one on each floor and if you live on one floor find a position that is near the bedroom. The batteries will need replacing every year and you must check the alarm every month to ensure it is working.

beauty treatments

home makeovers with paints, papers and tiles

Now that fashion relates to interiors as well as clothes, and the wrong floor covering can be just as much a gaffe as the wrong skirt length, knowing how to keep your decor up to date will allow you to entertain friends without fear of losing your fashion cred. You may not be able to afford architectural schemes and designer furniture but whether you favour minimalism or country chic, it is possible to create a sense of a style with paint and wallpaper and a little pruning and preening of your possessions.

Keeping it simple is wisest and easiest. Fortunately the simple, uncluttered look is currently very chic, but it also provides a good basis for a more decorative approach. Clearing out a room ready for decorating is an opportunity for a big clear-out of unwanted stuff and out-dated tat ready for a fresh look and perhaps a fresh start. Favourite belongings will come in to their own when placed in a newly decorated environment and it will be easier to throw away those that don't show up so well.

Preparation is important if you want to achieve a good finish. Filling in holes, washing and rubbing down old paintwork can be tedious (and not as much fun as the actual painting or papering), but it is satisfying and produces a more professional-looking result. Paint is easy to use, especially emulsion which can be put on quickly with a roller or large brush. Eco-friendly, water-based gloss and eggshell finishes are now available which are much easier to use, are less smelly than the spirit-based versions and, as an added bonus, the brushes can be washed out in water. Wallpapering may not be quite so easy as slapping on paint but it isn't difficult if you stick to one wall or uncomplicated spaces. It is useful for covering up a particularly bad surface and wallpaper is making a comeback – look out for new designs by trendy designers and re-vamped fifties retro styles.

It is quite possible to change the whole character of your home with a single tin of paint so be adventurous – you can always paint over it if you hate it. Try out some of the fabulous colours on those tempting paint charts and impress trend-conscious visitors by regularly re-painting a wall in the latest fashionable hue. A coat of paint not only freshens an interior but can be used to unify and create an illusion of space. Several small rooms will feel part of a single space if they are painted the same colour, and a collection of different style chairs will look like a set if given the same treatment. Bold colours add drama and focus while patterned wallpaper can bring a touch of retro or romance.

Even the most uninspiring environment can be improved by a little tender loving care. A lick of paint can bring light into a dark room or a feeling of intimacy in a large space. It can also turn perfectly ordinary home into a wild wonderland so don't be timid, have a go!

essential paint equipment

Painting methods vary depending on the type of paint used and the finish required.

paintbrushes

Paintbrushes come in all sorts of shapes, sizes, types of bristle and prices. The very cheapest brushes – often sold in bargain sets – will shed their bristles and won't hold the paint well so are best avoided. The most expensive have high-quality, densely packed bristles for ease of application and a smooth finish, but unless you are planning a lot of decorating (and are prepared to take great care of your brushes) go for a medium price range. Check that the bristles spring back when you bend them. Real bristle is the best as each hair tapers naturally to a point, but good-quality synthetic bristles are perfectly fine.

If you intend to use a brush for painting your walls invest in a good-quality flat, 150-mm (6-inch) wide emulsion paintbrush. A range of narrow brushes will be needed for window frames and architraves and a slightly wider brush for larger areas of woodwork, such as doors. Narrow cutting-in brushes have the bristles cut at an angle to make it easier to get right to the edge when painting glazing bars.

paint rollers

Rollers are fantastic for covering large areas of wall or ceiling quickly and evenly. They consist of a roller 'sleeve' which fits on to a metal rod or wire cage attached to a handle. Most sleeves are either sheepskin (real or synthetic) or foam. Long-pile sheepskin holds a lot of paint but medium-pile is more manageable. Foam sleeves are less efficient as they tend to leave air bubbles on the surface.

Rollers are used with a tray – usually plastic but sometimes metal, which have a ribbed area which slopes down to a paint reservoir. Roller and tray sets are often very inexpensive and although the quality may not be tip-top, you can just throw them away after use. If, however, you are more ecologically minded, buy a good-quality set and wash thoroughly after use – replacement sleeves are available.

Long-handled roller extensions are available for painting ceilings and floors, which makes the job easier, and other sizes and shapes can be found including a small roller on a long handle for painting behind radiators, shaped rollers for painting into corners and small dense foam rollers for use with gloss or eggshell paint for large flat areas such as doors and bath panels.

paint pads

Paint pads are very useful for painting large flat areas and are generally thought to be as good as a roller. Rectangular in shape, they consist of a layer of short mohair pile attached to a foam layer, which gives flexibility and keeps the pad in contact with uneven surfaces. The pad is fixed to a plastic frame with an inte- grated handle. Also sold in sets with a tray, the best type of tray has a loading roller to ensure the paint is distributed evenly on the pad.

paint kettles

Paint kettles are plastic or metal pots with a handle into which you decant a smaller, more manageable amount of paint when you are using a brush. Especially useful if you are on a ladder.

dust sheets

Painting is a messy business so make sure you have enough dust sheets to protect furniture, floors and other sur- faces from paint splashes and the water and debris from washing and stripping down walls. Old sheets and bedspreads are ideal but use plastic sheeting under- neath on vulnerable surfaces as big blobs of paint will soak through fabric.

masking tape

Masking tape is perfect for keeping paint off glass when painting window frames and paint off carpet when painting skirt- ing boards. Use to get a straight edge for different coloured panels and borders.

preparation

Using the right tools makes preparation easier as well as more effective.

scrapers
Used for removing wallpaper or paint they have flat, non-flexible blades.

spokeshaves
Useful for removing paint from awkward corners and mouldings.

wallpaper scorers
Used to puncture the surface of coated or painted wallpaper.

steam strippers
A steam plate, held against the wall to penetrate the paper. Can be hired.

hot-air strippers
Heat and soften solvent-based paint so that it can be scraped off easily.

liquid paint strippers
Will break down the adhesive bond between wallpaper and the wall.

scrubbing brushes
Useful for cleaning dirt from corners.

wire brushes
Will remove flakes of paint or rust but can be a bit harsh so use with care.

dry paintbrushes
Can be used as dusting brushes to clean corners and keyholes.

preparing paintwork

When decorating, the end result will look better and last longer if you do a proper job of making good the old before adding the new. The thought of stripping the walls and rubbing down paintwork may fill you with dread, but it can become a cleansing experience for your mind as well as your home. Take out unwanted fixtures and fittings, but keep things that would be expensive or difficult to replace. If possible, strip walls back to bare plaster to provide a good surface for painting or papering and to reveal any cracks or damp problems.

preparing walls and ceilings

Stripping wallpaper can be hard work, but there are ways to make it easier. Choose a discreet corner and remove a small amount of wallpaper to gain an idea of how many layers there are, what type of paper it is, whether it will come away easily and the state of the wall underneath. If large amounts of plaster come away with the paper, it may be best to leave well alone and paint over the paper. Alternatively, get a builder in to re-plaster.

Uncoated paper should come off easily with wallpaper stripper mixed with warm water. Apply generously with a sponge until the paper can be scraped off. Repeat as many times as necessary. Steaming is also a very efficient way to remove wallpaper. Coated wallpapers, or paper that has been painted over, will need scoring with a wallpaper scorer or the edge of a scraper to allow the

stripper solution to soak through. If the paper is vinyl coated you can usually remove it by simply lifting the corners of the vinyl and pulling it away from its backing paper, which can then be removed with wallpaper stripper.

Once you have stripped the old wallpaper, remove any blobs of old paint, debris and dirt with a scraper then wash down the walls thoroughly before painting or re-papering. Use warm soapy water or a solution of sugar soap and finish with a sponge or cloth rinsed frequently in clean water. If the old paint surface is rough with loose flakes of paint use a wet-and-dry abrasive paper (dry sanding produces too much dust) to smooth the edges. Alternatively flat nylon scourers will scrub off any loose bits of paint and smooth down the surface. If, after filling in the holes and cracks (as described in the previous chapter), the surface still looks a bit flaky you can give the wall a coat of PVA bonding diluted in water to seal the surface – just follow the instructions on the tin. Paint and wallpaper adhesive will not adhere to old distemper so brush away any loose material and apply a stabilising primer. If the underlying paint is gloss or eggshell, it will be necessary to wash down the wall with sugar-soap (or similar) and then rub down with a medium wet-and-dry abrasive paper. To seal new or newly revealed bare plaster, dilute the first coat of paint (half paint, half water) or apply a coat of PVA as above. Put one coat of paint on the wall before

filling all the holes as some may not show once they have been painted over.

If, despite priming, rubbing down and using filling techniques, the wall surface is still uneven, you can either learn to love the 'distressed' effect or apply extra coats of paint with a roller to form a slightly textured finish that will soften the blemishes. Alternatively, cover the entire wall with lining paper (use a thick, textured variety for very uneven surfaces) which can then be painted.

Cover stains such as damp or mildew with a stain block or recommended primer, but address the source of the stain first to prevent the stains reappearing. Also, covering damp with an impervious coating will only send the moisture elsewhere where it could do more damage.

preparing woodwork

Prepare old woodwork for repainting by washing down and keying the surface using warm water and sugar soap or detergent. A flat nylon scourer is good for getting rid of blemishes and will also help break down the surface. Pay particular attention to skirting boards, which are often scuffed, the areas around door handles and window catches, which will be greasy, and make sure you get into all corners, especially on window frames. Sand down any old drips and wrinkles. Hard gloss paint may need further rubbing down with fine wet-and-dry abrasive paper. Repair chips and damaged areas with primer, building up the surface with several coats if necessary, rubbing down between each. Wipe down with a clean cloth dipped in white spirit to get rid of any remaining dust and grease.

If possible, paint over the existing paint as stripping it off is a messy, time-consuming business. However, if the old paint surface is really bad, or the build-up of paint is the cause of ill-fitting windows and doors, stripping might be necessary.

A hot-air stripper softens paint so it can be scraped off easily, often several coats in one go. The nozzle is held about 50mm (2in) from the surface and moved slowly back and forth until the paint blisters. Remove the paint with a scraper or shavehook. Different shaped nozzles can be used to focus the heat or diffuse it and, on narrow glazing bars, will keep heat away from the glass.

If you think this sounds scary the alternative is to use a chemical paint stripper, which is no picnic either. Follow the instructions carefully, allow plenty of ventilation, wear a mask to protect against the fumes, and wear good protective gloves as the stripper will burn your skin on contact. Strippers usually consist of a thick viscous liquid that is dabbed onto the paint until it blisters. How easy this is depends on how many layers of paint there are. It is better to keep applying more stripper until it has penetrated all the layers and the paint (or most of it) can be scraped off in one go. Liquid paint strippers are not suitable for use on large areas as the fumes are too overpowering. If you are stripping paint ready for repainting, some residue will not be a problem as long as it is rubbed down and free of grease. But if you want to strip down to the bare wood you will have to work very hard to get every bit off, using chemical paint stripper or a combination of this and a hot-air stripper.

lead paint

Until the 1960s, lead was widely used in solvent-based paints and primers. Removing these paints can be hazardous as dust containing lead particles can be inhaled and absorbed through the skin. You are advised to obtain a leaflet about this before tackling your woodwork (ring or visit the website of the Health and Safety Executive). If possible, leave existing lead paint in place, smooth any surface defects with wet-and-dry abrasive paper or wire wool dampened with white spirit and simply paint over it. If it is necessary to remove old paint, avoid dust by using a chemical paint stripper rather than a dry abrasive or use a hot-air stripper set at a low temperature to avoid the release of toxic fumes. Wear protective clothing and a facemask. Any exposed skin should be washed thoroughly afterwards and the room should also be washed down with water and detergent. All peelings should be collected and placed in a sealed bag. A domestic vacuum cleaner is not powerful enough to remove all lead traces in dust and paint flakes so hire an industrial-standard vacuum cleaner.

primers and sealers

Some surfaces may need special treatment in order to make them suitable for painting.

stabilising primer

A white or clear liquid used on walls to bind dusty, powdery and flaky surfaces.

wood primer

Available in solvent-based, water-based, acrylic or aluminium forms. Used on new or bare wood to seal and prevent subsequent applications of paint soaking into the wood.

general-purpose primer

Used for wood, metal and plaster as well as porous building materials. Look out for water-based versions.

metal primer

Prevents corrosion and provides a key for paint. Rust inhibitors also available.

PVA bonding agent

A liquid adhesive which, when diluted, can be used as a primer and sealer.

stain sealer

Prevents stains bleeding through paint.

undercoat

A matt coating used on woodwork to cover primer and minor imperfections. Provides a smooth, dense surface for topcoats. Particularly effective if the topcoat is a dark colour or high gloss finish.

essential points about paint

For a fraction of the price of a Prada handbag you can completely transform your room, and perhaps even your life. If you like to change your interior style as frequently as your clothes, then a coat of paint will do it.

it's colourful
Paint comes in the proverbial 'bewildering' variety of colours, but there are lots of specialist and designer paint ranges which can help you make up your mind by selecting and combining all the latest, must-have colours.

it's confusing
It always used to be gloss or eggshell paint for woodwork and emulsion for walls, but now you can buy paint in all sorts of finishes as well as colours – from glamorous satin and glitter paints to posh flat-oil finishes and distemper.

it's easy
Water-based paints are easy to use. It is not too difficult to produce a nice even finish especially if you use a roller. Some paints guarantee to cover in one coat and come ready-to-use in a tray with a roller or pad so you just have to peel the lid off and paint away.

it's messy
Paint rollers may be efficient at covering walls but they will also cover your hair, face, spectacles and unsuspecting pets. Over-filled brushes cover your hands and arms while solvent-based paints are thicker, stickier and hard to remove from unwanted areas.

it's worth it
Paint can change the look and mood of a room making it look cleaner, bigger, cosier, sexier, smarter or just nicer. It is a well-known fact that when selling a property, a coat of paint can turn your house from an ordinary dwelling into a desireable residence.

it's tricky
Painting woodwork is more fiddly than walls; smaller areas take longer to paint as you must use a finer brush. New wood will need a coat of primer first and then, ideally, an undercoat. Gloss, eggshell, satin, and the new flat finishes need careful application to avoid drips and sags.

it's quick
Using emulsion paint and a roller it is possible to cover a huge area of wall in a very short time. Even with a brush it doesn't take too long. Modern paints dry quickly so you can put on the next coat in as little as two hours and finish a whole room in a morning.

it's slow
Solvent-based paints not only take longer to apply, they also take longer to dry. You may have to wait up to 24 hours before putting on the next coat. For a perfect finish, you may also have to rub down the surface between coats which can take ages.

types of paint

Buying paint used to be simple: you used water-based emulsion for walls and solvent-based gloss (or eggshell if you were daring) for woodwork. Nowadays we are presented with not only a vast range of colours, but also a confusing selection of types and finishes from the cheerfully cheap to the ultra chic. They do, however divide fairly logically into paints for walls and paints for woodwork.

Walls are mostly painted with emulsion which is water-based, while woodwork, which needs a harder, more durable surface, has traditionally been painted with solvent-based paints. However, the demand for paints that are easy to apply, dry quickly and are eco-friendly, has led to the development of many more water-based paints and primers that are suitable for use on wood and metal.

It is important to read what it says on the tin. All information on contents, safety precautions, preparation, application, drying times, coverage and how to clean equipment is normally printed on the tin together with any special requirements or features.

paint for walls

Paint provides a pick-me-up for tired walls which can be transformed in an afternoon.

emulsion

A water-based emulsion is best for walls. It is easy to apply and to wash out of brushes, rollers, and your hair. It is available in a matt or silk finish. One-coat emulsions are available in a limited range of colours and often come in a tray ready for rollering. They often have additives such as vinyl to give a smoother, more stable, durable and washable surface. Emulsion can be applied with a brush, roller or pad. As well as being easy to use, emulsion is readily available in a huge range of colours. What's more, it is quick drying – further coats can be applied in 2–4 hours – and has minimal smell.

distemper

Distemper consists of pigments and binders (glues and natural resins) dispersed in water and must be used correctly in order to achieve an even finish. Usually produced by specialist companies, distemper varies in type and composition so always follow all instructions on the tin. It can be applied on top of existing emulsion, but bare plaster will require several thin coats. Its dense, chalky finish is historically correct and particularly suited to old properties. It is especially good for mouldings which become clogged and lose definition if painted with standard emulsions. However, distemper is less stable than emulsion and will rub off, so it is unsuitable for areas of high wear such as staircases. Apply with a brush or, on delicate or fragile plasterwork, a spray. It looks wonderful, but if you are after a quick fix this isn't the paint for you.

other paints

There are several 'special effect' paints on the market but the effect is not always successful and they do require certain application skills. Simple is best, and smart girls will keep it plain.

paint for woodwork

Freshly painted woodwork provides the finishing touch to a room.

gloss

Gloss has a hard-wearing finish with a reflective surface quality. It shows up all imperfections and needs careful application to avoid sags and drips. For best results, use over an undercoat. Traditionally gloss is solvent-based and therefore smelly and slow to dry, but water-based versions now available. One-coat gloss saves time but can look a bit thin. Non-drip gloss is cleaner but can be a bit glutinous and difficult to apply. If used with an undercoat a single topcoat of gloss is usually sufficient. Solvent-based gloss require up to 16 hours drying time and will not fully harden for several days.

other paints

Eggshell, satin and soft sheen all have a slightly reflective surface quality and are available in several finishes from soft sheen to matt. Much easier to use than gloss, they won't show up every imperfection. Use with an undercoat to get a denser colour. Water-based are now widely available. Flat paint has a dead matt finish. It can also be used on plaster and papered walls. The versions produced by specialist companies are usually oil-based.

how much paint?

The amount of paint required for a job will depend on the type and make of paint, the colour, the state and porosity of the existing surface and the method of application. Commercially produced emulsions are generally quite thick and will cover well, though some brands, and cheaper paints, are thinner. Some specialist paints will need extra coats as their ingredients tend to have fewer additives which aid coverage. Details of estimated coverage will be printed on the tin – usually in square metres per litre or per can. The average coverage of 5 litres of emulsion is between 60–65 square metres (645–700 square feet) but, as discussed above, this will vary. Extra coats will be necessary if you are covering a dark colour or pattern. Pure, deep colours, such as bright yellows or reds, will need extra coats to achieve an even depth of colour and this will normally be indicated on the tin.

Rollers are fast and will cover in fewer, thicker coats. The brush method is slower but tends to use less paint than rollering as it is a little more controlled. Make sure you buy enough paint to do the whole room. Different batches of paint will differ slightly and if you are using a colour mixing service bear in mind that the amounts of colour dispensed can vary slightly each time the colour is mixed, and that machines in different stores will rarely produce an exact match.

applying paint

How you decide to apply your paint will depend not only on the paint but also on your personality. If you want fast results you will love using a roller, but if you are a bit of a perfectionist and enjoy art then the pleasure of the brush may appeal. Whichever method you choose, remember to unscrew all light switches, fittings and sockets so that you can paint behind for a neater appearance.

using a paint roller

Before painting walls and ceilings you'll have to do a bit of 'cutting in' which involves using a small brush to paint round all the edges – ceiling/wall joins, corners, skirting boards, light switches and light fittings – as well as the narrow areas where a roller won't fit. Pour paint into the deep end of the roller tray so that it comes up to the level of the end of the slope. Choose a roller no more than 225mm (9in) long (anything bigger becomes too tiring to use). Load the roller by dipping it into the paint and then rolling it up and down on the ribbed section to distribute the paint evenly (with a clean, dry roller you may have to do this several times). Place the roller on the surface, using enough pressure to prevent it spinning round on its own, and transfer the paint to the wall. Keep the roller in contact with the surface at all times, distributing the paint evenly in all directions, but don't try to cover too large an area with one load as the coverage will be too thin and may lead to an uneven, patchy

finish. Try not to overload the paint roller as this will increase the spottle count. Use a long handle attachment for painting ceilings – but wear a hat!

Small rollers are great for applying eggshell or gloss paint onto large areas such as doors, but keep to one direction for your finishing strokes.

using a paint pad

Using a paint pad is much the same as using a roller but the paint is loaded evenly by passing it over a roller integrated into the paint tray. Keep the pad flat against the surface and paint in all directions using a gentle sweeping action.

using a paintbrush

Applying thick paint with a brush is hard work and it is sometimes easier to thin down the paint slightly and apply extra coats. It is important not to overload the brush as this leads to messy painting (and paint running down your arms) so dip only a third of the bristle area into the paint and wipe off any excess on the side of the tin before painting. How you hold the brush will depend on personal preference and comfort as well as the size of the brush and the type of paint. Holding it like a pen will give more control and makes sense for narrow brushes on woodwork, but for wide brushes (especially on ceilings) it may feel more comfortable if you hold the handle firmly in your fist. The most important thing is to transfer the paint onto the surface in ver-

tical strokes – not dabs or sploshes – and spread it out using horizontal strokes as well. On large areas don't brush out too thinly at the edges as you will get an uneven finish. Work from right to left if you are right-handed (the other way round if you are left-handed) so that your arm is away from your body.

For woodwork, especially solvent-based paints and gloss finishes, the brushstrokes should follow the grain of the wood and be vertical or horizontal (according to the direction of the frame or skirting board) to prevent brushmarks spoiling the finished surface.

To get a neat line along skirting boards, around door and window frames, and between ceilings and wall, place the brush a short distance away from the edge and press down so that the bristles fan out to reach the edge. If you can't do this without losing control of the brush, paint or your temper, then use masking tape. It is, however, always a good idea to use masking tape around the edges of the glass when painting window frames. A variety of simple plastic shields are available to keep paint off floors and glass, but as they need to be held in position they can get in the way and prevent you using your spare hand for something more useful, like holding paint.

All brushes shed a few bristles when they are new so before using them on woodwork (where shedding bristles will be a great nuisance and spoil the finish) break them in by using with emulsion first.

perfect paintwork

As long as you prepare surfaces properly and take reasonable care when applying paint the finished result should look fine. Small defects and slightly imperfect finishes rarely stand out once the furniture is in place. Woodwork needs more attention than walls. For a very beautiful, high-quality finish on woodwork apply two or three topcoats, rubbing down with wire wool or wet-and-dry abrasive paper between each coat. Follow instructions on the tin and don't allow the paint to fully harden before re-coating.

avoiding common problems

drips, runs and sags Make sure there is not too much paint on your brush/roller and brush it out across the surface.

brushmarks Use a good-quality brush and make sure it is perfectly clean. Brush out runs as you go along but don't attempt to brush them out once the surface has started to dry.

specks and lumps on the surface Make sure your brush is clean and that the surface is completely free from dirt and dust, including the corners. During a break put the lids back on tins and put brushes, rollers or pads (complete with their trays) inside a plastic bag, tied or folded, to stop them drying out and attracting dust and dirt.

flaking Ensure that you have prepared the surface properly by getting rid of all loose material and grease spots. Once you have washed down the walls make sure they are dry before you begin to paint.

poor finish Remember to score the surface before painting and allow sufficient drying time between coats. Check your paint is not being applied too thinly and apply enough coats for the material.

patchy finish Paint in mainly vertical strokes to get good coverage and only take a break when an entire wall is complete. For a good finish with gloss on doors paint the last strokes vertically.

cleaning up

The worst thing about decorating is cleaning up afterwards. If you have been a diligent painter it should just be a matter of folding away the dust sheets (taking care not to shake dust onto still-wet paint) and standing back to admire your work. However, there are usually a few stray splashes and spottles which should be cleaned off immediately with a damp cloth (or a cloth soaked in white spirit if the paint is solvent-based) while bigger blobs can be removed with a scraper. Be careful not to disturb soft paint and don't try to neaten up edges until the paint is hard.

Try to wash brushes and other equipment as soon as you have finished as the paint will harden and be more difficult to remove. If this isn't possible then put them in a plastic bag or leave them to soak in plenty of water. If you have been using water-based paints wash brushes, rollers and pads in plenty of warm soapy water and rinse until the water is clear. Flex the bristles of brushes to make sure no paint remains in the roots. Squeeze or shake out surplus moisture and leave to dry naturally. For solvent-based paints wipe off excess paint on newspaper then flex the bristles in a jar of white spirit (or special thinner as indicated on the tin) to dissolve the remaining paint. Wash with hot soapy water and rinse. Repeat if necessary until the brush is clean. Keep paintbrushes in shape by folding paper around the bristles and securing with a rubber band.

paint projects

With the availability of a huge range of paints and palettes to suit all personalities, it is up to you to decide whether to be restrained or go for drama and adventure. Inspiration can come from a variety of sources – a postcard, a trip to a museum or gallery, a bunch of flowers or just the desire to add a little more colour to your life.

white space

If you long for large white, light-filled spaces but your own home is somewhat confined, clear out your clutter and paint your walls, ceiling, floor, woodwork and even furniture in fresh, clean, dazzling white.

dash of drama

Use shiny gloss for drama, glamour and hard-edged modernism. Paint a whole room in a bright colour but keep furnishings to a minimum. Alternatively, paint just one wall or a single panel – use masking tape for a perfect edge, and leave a gap round the edges for more impact and neater joins. Use a contrasting colour for window and doorframes, and why not paint each door in a different, bright colour.

cool shades

Use combinations of hints, tints and tones of a single colour to add variety without contrast. Choose a collection of the new whites – from pale creams to greeny greys – for an amazingly subtle look. Or go for twiggy, pebbly colours to create an aura of natural harmony. Use lots of different colours but keep control by choosing similar moods or shades of each.

touch of history

The vogue for historical correctness has led to the development of new types of paint based on old 'recipes'. The colours are wonderfully flat and dense. They bring old properties back to life and give new places a sense of identity. The range of colours is limited but they share a similar quality which means they all work well together. Dark coloured woodwork looks contemporary as well as authentic.

essential points about wallcoverings

For the last few years, paint has been the favoured finish for walls especially with people who are more adventurous with colour. Wallpaper, however, is making a comeback. Blousy roses and spriggy flowers have never lost their appeal but the revival of interest in fifties and sixties design has brought bold geometrics back into the limelight. Even if you are a firm fan of plain walls, you may need to paper in order to provide a good surface on which to paint.

it's a cover-up

Obliterate cracked, lumpy, bumpy plaster with a covering of good thick paper which can be painted or exist in its own right. Bring a room back to life with a fresh layer of wallpaper on top of old, dirty, dated and impossible-to-remove paper. Lose imperfect edges, ugly features and funny angles in a riot of pattern.

it's tricky

Those endless comedy sketches can be played out for real in your own home as you wrestle with sticky paper which appears to have a mind of its own. Matching patterns, cutting round light fittings and getting it into awkward corners will test your ingenuity and natural good humour.

it's beautiful

There are lots of wonderful papers around including stunning designer ranges, hand-printed and historical patterns as well as fabric wallcoverings such as silk and the re-discovered hessian. A patterned room has a special quality and warmth that cannot be achieved using paint.

it's revealing

Thin paper will show up any small imperfections in the underlying surface and highlight larger ones in full technicolour glory. The wrong pattern and colour can make a small room even smaller and a large room difficult to furnish. Wobbly walls and less-than-straight edges will be emphasised by stripes or large patterns.

it's unsuitable

Damp walls are not good for wallpaper unless you can waterproof the surface beforehand with PVA or special sealer. Unless paper is coated the surface will rub off in areas of high wear such as halls and staircases. Furniture will also damage the surface if allowed to come into contact. Porous and non-colour fast papers are not suitable for kitchens or bathrooms or anywhere where they may come into contact with moisture.

it's easy

New types of papers and pastes make life easier, and providing you take your time, follow the rules, use the right equipment, and keep calm, there is no reason why you shouldn't derive enormous pleasure from transforming ugly walls into beautiful surfaces, and ordinary rooms into stunning spaces.

types of wallcoverings

Putting wallpaper on the wall can be a lot easier and much more fun than getting it off. New products and methods as well as new, stunning designs have made wall-papering a lot more tempting than it used to be so why not be bold, and have a go.

lining paper

Plain, buff-coloured paper used over slightly uneven or impervious surfaces to create a suitable paint surface. Also used underneath heavy or dear wallcoverings.

woodchip

Made by sandwiching particles of wood between two layers of paper. Inexpensive and easy to hang, it covers poor plaster and uneven surfaces. Should be painted.

textured-relief papers

Heavily embossed with a variety of patterns, from the traditional designs used extensively in the Victorian and Edwardian eras to more modern and abstract versions. Rarely used on every wall, more often used below a dado rail, or on a ceiling. Always painted. Emulsion is fine but eggshell and gloss is more hardwearing and looks more historically accurate. New, simpler, contemporary designs now available of a quite different character from 'authentic' designs.

printed papers

An enormous range of designs and colours from small spriggy flowers to bold geometrics and famous designs from the past. The thickness and quality varies and will be reflected in the price.

ready-pasted papers

Some wallcoverings are pre-coated with an adhesive which is activated by soaking in cold water. Specially designed inexpensive plastic troughs are available for this process.

coated papers

A thin coating of PVA is applied to printed papers to create an impervious and washable surface for bathrooms and kitchens. Vinyl wallcoverings consist of a paper or cotton backing with the pattern printed onto a vinyl coating and fused into the surface using heat. These are durable, washable and colourfast and therefore ideally suited to bathrooms and kitchens. Often sold ready-pasted.

borders

Borders of varying designs and widths are often intended for use with a co-ordinating paper but can be used on their own on a painted wall. Some are ready-pasted.

vintage papers

A number of shops and market stalls have realised the interest in retro styles and sell rolls of original old wallpaper, especially from the fifties and sixties. It is rare to get any quantity but these can become a fabulous focus of an interior.

essential equipment

Cutting, pasting and handling lengths of wallpaper can be awkward and needs a clear space, patience, care and a sense of humour which you are more likely to retain if you invest in the right equipment.

fold-up pasting table

Cheap and very useful. It is the right size – a few millimetres wider than the average roll of paper, and a good working height – slightly higher than a dining table. It is light and can be moved around easily.

pasting brush

Apply paste with a large pasting brush or wall brush with soft, long bristles. Alternatively use a short-pile paint roller and put the paste in the tray.

paperhanger's scissors

These have extra long blades for straight cuts, but any large pair of sharp scissors will do.

paperhanger's brush

Looking like a wide paintbrush with the handle chopped off this is used for smoothing the paper on to the wall. The bristles must be soft enough not to damage the surface of the wallpaper, but stiff enough to be poked into corners and force out excess paste.

seam roller

Has a small wood or plastic roller which can be run up and down the seams to press down the paper so that it won't lift when dry. Rubber smoothing rollers squeeze trapped air from under the paper. Use a felt roller for more delicate papers.It is probably wise not to use a seam roller on textured paper.

retractable tape measure, plumb line and spirit level

Essential for helping you to mark the position of the paper.

wallpaper paste

Most pastes are in the form of powder or flakes ready to mix with water, although ready-mixed pastes are now available.

Standard all-purpose paste is suitable for light to medium-weight papers but can also be used in a less diluted form for hanging heavy papers.

Heavy-duty or ready-mixed paste is used for heavy, embossed papers and paper-backed fabrics.

Fungicidal paste prevents the growth of mould behind impervious papers.

Stain-free paste is used on delicate papers as conventional paste can stain.

applying wallpaper

If you are a complete DIY novice, think carefully before embarking on wallpapering a room. If the room is very large, has high ceilings, is very irregular in shape, or has more than one window and door, it would be wise call in a professional decorator to do it for you or stick to paint. For your first attempt why not paper just one feature wall or a narrow chimney breast, this way you avoid corners, overlaps and having to cut round light switches, etc. Alternatively start with a room that is very small with no awkward features. Unless you are doing a single wall it is best to stick to patterns that won't look obvious if they don't quite line up. Avoid ceilings if possible.

Wallpaper comes in fairly standard widths and lengths – approximately 1050 mm (33 feet) long and 530mm (21 inches) wide. To calculate how much you need, measure the wall height from ceiling to skirting board and add 100mm (4 inches) for trimming to get the length. Work out how many lengths you can get from one roll of wallpaper – four strips is the average. Measure round the perimeter of the room (ignoring windows and doors) to find out how many roll

widths you will need. Divide this by the number of lengths you can cut from one length to give the number of rolls required. Add to this an allowance for matching up any pattern (the repeat will be written on the label) and add a little more for possible mistakes and accidents. Look out for handy charts for calculating the number of rolls at DIY stores and decorating shops.

preparing walls
Prepare walls as for painting but seal newly plastered walls with a proprietary size or diluted wallpaper paste so that the wallpaper will stick. Finish painting ceilings and woodwork before applying wallpaper. Measure the length of wallpaper required adding 100mm (4 inches) top and bottom, for trimming. Mix up the wallpaper paste in a bucket. Cut several lengths, marking the top of each one, and lay them face down on the pasting table. With the edge of the top length along the side edge of the table, apply paste down the centre of the paper and brush out towards the front edge making sure the edges are well pasted. Slide the length across to the back edge of the

table and brush on more paste towards that edge making sure that edge is also well covered. Fold the pasted paper over onto itself then slide the paper along the table and repeat the process until the whole length is pasted.

things with string
To prevent the ends of cut lengths curling and getting in the way tuck them behind a length of string tied round the legs of the pasting table. Similarly, tie a piece of string across the middle of the paste bucket to rest the pasting brush on.

papering a room
If possible, start on a blank wall with no windows or doors. Beginning in one corner, work away from the window so you are not working in your own light. Measuring from the corner, use a plumb line or spirit level to mark a line on the wall that is 12mm ($\frac{1}{2}$ inch) less than the width of the roll (to allow for an overlap round the corner). Leaving the bottom half folded for easier handling, place the top of the pasted strip on the wall allowing the paper to overlap on to the ceiling by approximately 50mm (2 inches) and slide

it so that it aligns with the marked line. Use the paperhanger's brush to brush the paper on to the wall. Use gentle strokes and work from the middle outwards to squeeze out trapped air and excess paste. Run the tip of a scissor blade along the paper where it joins the ceiling, peel the paper away, cut off the excess then brush the paper back on to the wall. Unfold the rest of the strip and brush the rest of the paper onto the wall (making sure you push the paper into the corner) until you reach the skirting board where you trim as above. Wipe away excess paste as you go using a damp cloth.

Turn a corner by marking another line so that the paper covers the overlap. When you reach a door or window frame allow the length of wallpaper to fall across the door or window and make a diagonal cut. Brush the paper into place along the side of the frame then score with scissors, trim leaving 12mm (1/2 inch) along the top edge for the piece above the frame and brush back. Brush down remaining paper above the door and trim along the top of the frame as before.

papering techniques

starting in a corner

Brush seams to remove excess paste and finish with a seam roller.

papering round a window

For a neat edge around a window reveal, paper the top of the reveal separately, paper over the overlap and cut along the edge.

papering round a door

Make a diagonal cut, trim, brush into place around the frame and trim off any excess.

papering round a radiator and a lightswitch

Mark position of radiator bracket and cut from the bottom. Push paper into position around bracket using a long handled brush. Trim the diagonal cuts, unscrew the light switch, tuck paper behind and screw back into postion.

wallpaper projects

Wallpaper is back in fashion with new chic designs by established designers as well as a revival in nostalgic pretty prints. Plain painted walls can complement every interior style but wallpaper can be used for historic authenticity, as a fashion statement or to add a touch of luxury or indulgent femininity.

main feature

Papering a single wall is not only easier to do but also an opportunity to be adventurous. Choose a very bold or dramatic print that would otherwise swamp the room. Use it to set a style, a theme or just a colour story.

inside job

If you are a firm fan of plain walls but love wallpaper designs, put some on the inside of a cupboard or a chest. Surround your blouses with blousy roses, discipline your suits with stripes or cheer up your little black dresses with jazzy prints. Line drawers and boxes with pretty papers to keep delicate fabrics safe and make the contents feel loved.

indulge

Give in to your innermost desires and paper a
bedroom in pretty roses – you know you want to.
Use two or three different patterns in the same
colourway or use the same pattern in different
colours. Do the ceiling too. And put up matching
curtains if you dare. Convert a small dark room
into a salon with deep-coloured silky wallcoverings
and a few gold patterns. Go hippy with a riot of
patterns in bright colours or fill the bathroom with
ships and seagulls.

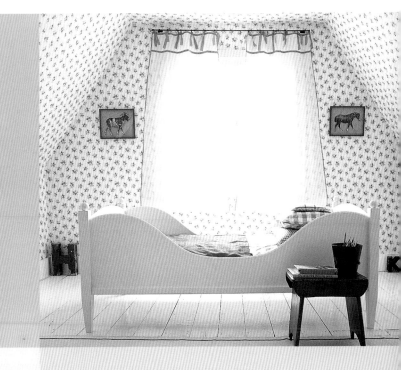

a bit of art

Create large modern paintings by pasting papers
onto hardboard 'canvases'. Prop them against
plain walls or hang them gallery-style. A good way
of appreciating those vintage panels you picked up
from the retro shop. Be really ironic and put them in
fancy gold frames.

essential points about tiles

Tiles give a crisp, clean and efficient finish in a kitchen or bathroom where their hard surface is practical, water-resistant and easy to clean. Their regular, even shape and finish makes them perfect for an architectural, minimal look whilst chunky and hand-painted tiles in glowing colours can be used to add warmth and character in any room.

they are practical...
Tiles are hard-wearing, waterproof, and easy to clean making them ideal for bathrooms, showers, kitchens and utility rooms.

they are easy to cut...
Making straight cuts on thin ceramic wall tiles is surprisingly easy using tile cutters and tile 'nibblers', and easier still with a platform cutter.

they are versatile...
Can be used on walls and floors but also on tables and worktops. Their colour and finish can set the look from hard-edged modern to hand-made ethnic.

they look good...
Crisp, clean, smooth and cool for a modern look. Soft, matt, warm and colourful for traditional or country style. Perfect when plain but pretty when patterned.

they are difficult to cut...
Curves must be cut nealty with a tile saw which is fiddly and difficult for an amateur. Thicker tiles need to be cut with an angle grinder, heavy-duty platform cutter or a power wet saw.

they are easy to keep clean...
Their hard surface repels dirt and any splashes can be wiped off with a damp cloth.

they look dreadful...
The uniformity of tiles emphasises bad workmanship but even if the tiles have been put up beautifully they will never look good if the colour or pattern is not to your taste.

they need cleaning often...
Clean tiles regularly, especially in a shower where a build up of soap will coat the tiles with a dull, scummy film.

types of tiles

There are now lots of specialist tile shops – have a good browse and be inspired!

ceramic tiles

Available in a variety of shapes and sizes, plain and patterned, shiny or matt. Most are square and the most common sizes are 100mm (4 inches) and 150mm (6 inches). Larger sizes and rectangular, octagonal and interlocking shapes are also available.

glazed tiles

Have a hard shiny coating of glaze which is waterproof and very durable.

unglazed tiles

Have a duller, matt finish and may need to be sealed to reduce porosity.

industrially-produced tiles

Usually quite thin and therefore easy to cut, and their machine made precision means the thickness, surface finish, colour and pattern is uniform and therefore they are easy to fit and match.

hand-made tiles

More irregular in shape and they are usually thicker than machine made tiles. The colour and finish will vary and patterns will be less precise which gives them more 'character'.

mosaic tiles

Small and give a different sort of look. Laying them individually would be very time consuming so several are either attached to mesh backing which remains in place after applying, or a paper covering which is removed once they are in place.

curved tiles

Most tiles sold now have straight edges on all sides but some have one curved, finished edge for neater edges on window cills and panels.

narrow border tiles

There are a number of narrow border tiles, many of them decorative and some with relief patterns. Small thin pencil tiles are available for edging.

mirror tiles

Fixed with self-adhesive pads (normally included with the tile) and are butted together with no gaps.

other materials

Most tiles are ceramic, but the popularity of stone and slate for floors has led to the development of thinner versions for walls. As a natural material they are not easy to cut and are best left to expert tilers.

equipment

For a professional finish make the most of the many new products for cutting and applying.

platform or tile cutter

Used to cut tiles in half. Platform cutter is easier and safer to use than the tile cutter, with which you have to score and snap by hand.

tile nibblers

Pincers used to cut narrow strips, small notches and corners.

tile saw

Used for cutting out curved shapes when fitting tiles round pipes, etc.

metal file, tile sander and oiled slip stone

Used to smooth down cut edges.

tile adhesive

Usually sold ready-mixed and most are water-resistant.

spacers

Guides for spacing tiles accurately.

grout

Fills gaps between tiles. Supplied in powder form to be mixed with water. Heat-resistant versions for kitchens and epoxy-based versions for germ-free worktops are available.

plastic edging strip

Makes corners and edges of tiling neater; protects them from chips.

preparing walls for tiling

Before deciding to try your hand at tiling look carefully at the area to be tiled. If possible avoid having to tile round windows, fittings, pipes and awkward recesses. Don't be too ambitious, stick to small areas such as behind a worktop or a basin. Industrially-produced tiles will be easier to use as they are uniform in size and shape and are not too thick. However, as hand-made tiles are irregular in shape, slightly irregular spacing and an even surface will not show too much!

how many tiles?

It is not too difficult to calculate the number of tiles needed. Work out how many of your chosen tiles will be needed for the height and the width of the area to be covered, multiply the two figures and add 10 per cent (perhaps 15 per cent for beginners) for breakages and mistakes.

preparing surfaces

Tiles can be stuck to most surfaces as long as they are flat, clean and dry with no loose paint, plaster or debris. New plaster should be left for several weeks in order to dry out properly. Don't tile over wallpaper. Taking off old tiles is a messy and laborious business but fortunately you can tile on top. Scrape out any loose grout, stick down any loose tiles and fill any big gaps with filler. Prepare unstable surfaces with a coat of PVA based adhesive but make sure it is the waterproof variety.

marking out

Make a tiling gauge by laying out a row of tiles with spacers in between each one and carefully marking the position of each tile on a long (straight) piece of 50mm (2 inches) wide softwood battening. Use this to plan where the tiles should go. The layout needs to be worked out carefully so that the amount of cutting is kept to a minimum, so stick to whole tiles wherever possible. If the tiles span the whole wall don't start at one side as walls are rarely straight and you may end up with gaps that are impossible to fill in. Position the first whole tile away from the edge and check each side to make sure that the cut tiles at either edge are of roughly even width – draw a vertical line down the centre and work out from this.

applying tiles

The most difficult part of tiling is cutting them to fit around objects and into corners. However, the availability of good, reasonably-priced tile cutters and a few tips will make this a less daunting prospect.

simple tiling techniques

For splashbacks or small panels choose a depth based on numbers of whole tiles so that you don't have to cut the bottom row. Mark out the first horizontal row of tiles, using a spirit level to make sure they are straight. For extra accuracy and easy positioning, fix battens along the side and bottom as a frame against which the tiles can be placed.

Apply adhesive to the wall using a notched spreader to make it easier to position and bed the tile. Do no more than 1 square metre (1 square yard) at a time to avoid the adhesive drying out. Position the first tile in the corner formed by the two battens if you are using them.

Always start with a whole tile. Press the tile into place until it feels firm. Using spacers as you go, continue working in rows, adding more adhesive as required and wiping away excess with a damp sponge. Allow 12 hours before removing the battens. Finish by filling in with the cut tiles. Make sure crosshead spacers do not protrude above the surface or they will stick out above the grout.

tile projects

mind the gap

Use different coloured grout to give an unexpected or ultra smart effect. Use grey with white tiles, or vice versa, for a subtler look. Using a similar colour grout and tiles will make the gaps 'disappear' while a contrasting colour with darker tones will look dramatic.

colour theory

For subtle variation use two close tones in alternating rows or in a chequerboard pattern. Or be very bold and use contrasting colours. Hand-made tiles give a wonderful melange of colour – look out for warm provencal yellows and moroccan tiles in vibrant turquoise.

reflected glory

Use mirror tiles in a bathroom for an all-round view or tile a panel or narrow strip in a bedroom or dressing room. Reflect light into a dark passageway with a strategically placed panel of mirror tiles.

shaping up

Rectangular tiles are very chic. Use them lengthways, laid in a brick-like pattern or, try them different ways up for something completely different. Make thin stripes across or down unexciting walls.

border control

Add interest with a row of tiles in a contrasting colour or texture along the top and sides of a tiled panel. Narrow rectangular tiles in plain colours are smart, and a single row of pencil tiles in the same colour will look minimal.

table talk

Cheer up a dull table or cupboard top with a brightly coloured tiled top (use a flexible adhesive and grout). Use any bits of broken tile if you don't want to buy new especially for this and create a mad mosaic. Place a collection of loose tiles in the centre of a dinner table for added decoration and a perfect surface for hot dishes.

mixing it

Go wild with mixed colours and patterns. Use rough or old tiles picked up from markets and skips to add a surprise element to plain walls or to design a whole patchwork wall.

tiling techniques

tiling a simple splashback

Measure and mark out the position of the tiles and, using a batten as a guide, work in rows starting in a top corner.

When tiling in a recess or lining the tiles up exactly with the edge of units mark the centre line and work out to the edges.

tiling behind units

For tiled areas that extend beyond and around units, place a batten along the side and along the line of the bottom of the lowest whole tile. Place the first tile where these battens join.

Take away the battens before measuring, cutting and positioning the final margin tiles.

cutting and fitting margin tiles

Fit margin tiles after all the whole tiles have been put on and mark each one individually as the edges of the wall may not be straight. To work out the size place a tile face down, on top of the neighbouring tile and against the edge of the wall or skirting board. Mark along the edge of the tile not forgetting to make an allowance for the spacing. Spread adhesive on the back of each filler tile and press into position.

grouting tiles

Allow 24 hours for the adhesive to harden. Using a rubber-bladed spreader or a piece of dense foam sponge, spread grout in all directions forcing it into all the gaps. Wipe grout from the surface of the tiles using a barely damp sponge. When the grout has dried polish the tiles with a dry cloth.

finishing off

Unless you have used tiles with a curved edge, grout around exposed edges to form a smooth join with the wall surface.

applying mosaic tiles

Mosaic tiles are normally supplied in sheets on a mesh backing or with a facing paper which is removed after application. Use the same adhesives and grouting as standard ceramic tiles but make sure that the gap left around each set of tiles is the same as the gap between the individual tiles. In order to make sure the tiles are bedded properly apply pressure with a piece of board covered in a soft material such as carpet, and tap gently with a wooden mallett. Fill in the margins by cutting strips, or single tiles from the sheet using tile nibblers to cut to size.

sealing gaps and edges

If the tiles are immediately above a sink, basin or bath don't grout the adjacent seal. Instead fill it with flexible silicone sealant. This is sold in plastic tubes with a pointed nozzle, some need to be used with a mastic gun but others can be squeezed by hand. Before application make sure the surface is dry and wipe with methylated spirit to get rid of any grease. Squeeze an even bead of sealant along the join. It takes a steady hand and steady pressure to get a good finish, do it all in one movement as joins will show. A strip of masking tape will help get a straight edge. Smooth the surface with a finger dipped in a 50/50 solution of water and washing up liquid.

tiling around a light switch

Fit margin tiles after all the whole tiles have been put on and mark each one individually as the edges of the wall may not be straight. To work out the size place a tile face down, on top of the neighbouring tile and against the edge of the wall or skirting board. Mark along the edge of the tile not forgetting to make an allowance for the spacing. Spread adhesive on the back of each filler tile and press into position.

tiling round a socket

Unscrew the socket, postion tile and mark position of socket allowing for an overlap but making sure the screw holes are not covered. Screw socket back after grouting is finished and dry.

cutting a margin tile

Place a whole tile upside down on top of a tile in the last row of whole, fixed tiles and position it against the finished edge. Allowing for the space between the tiles and, if necessary, grout between the edge of the wall or skirting board, mark the edge of the tile and use these marks to cut to size.

grouting tiles

Spread grout in all directions making sure to cover any spacers. After it has dried wipe off any remaining grout with a soft, dry cloth.

applying mosaic tiles

A mesh backing or facing paper makes mosaic tiling easier. Keep the spaces between the sheets of mosaic the same as the space between individual tiles. Use a carpet covered pad and a wooden mallet to bed the tiles into the adhesive.

off-the-peg or tailor-made

tackling self assembly or home-made furnishings

Now you have a neat, trim, freshly decorated interior the fun can really start. You will, of course, have edited your clutter so only the items that are good, useful or well-loved remain, so now comes the opportunity to organise and arrange your possessions to transform your living space into a visually pleasing, convenient and comfortable environment. Create your own personal style using a combination of colour, simple DIY and a few new purchases. Fortunately there is a wide and wonderful choice of products on the market and even if your budget is modest it is still possible to buy simple, well-designed furniture and furnishings to make your home stunning and stylish or just peaceful and calm, according to your personality or lifestyle.

The design, choice and quality of flat-pack furniture has never been better. Despite the often mystifying (or non-existent) assembly instructions, patience and a positive attitude will eventually be rewarded with a good looking, useful item to enhance your home.

The problem of finding somewhere to store or display all your possessions is often solved by the ever-useful shelf. The ability to put up shelves is a skill no self-respecting, modern, emancipated female should be without. Adding shelves in cupboards, wardrobes and alcoves too will maximise the use of space and enable you to store things efficiently or display them beautifully.

Making your own furniture may require advanced carpentry techniques but a trip to the DIY store can inspire innovative, easy-to-make ideas. Invest in sets of castors and allow your imagination to run away by fixing them on to slabs of wood or ready-made doors to make a roll-along occasional table or a bed base.

The variety of curtain poles, wires and fittings has made covering windows a lot more straightforward, and the fashion for simple panels and blinds require only straight lines and basic sewing skills. The huge range of ready-made blinds require only the use of a power drill and a screwdriver to install and give a room a clean, modern feel. If you are feeling adventurous, employ your knowledge of attaching hinges and fixing battens to make your own made-to-measure shutters.

Use your decorating skills to cheer up old unsightly furniture and bring it into line with the rest of the decor or to give that flat-pack a professional finish. Scour the second-hand furniture shops and antique markets for solid but quirky items, getting out your tool box to carry out a little repair and restoration or turn them into something completely different with the addition of a few bits and bobs and a dash of inventiveness.

getting it together

Knowing that you can pop along to the local furniture store, pick up enough items to fill a small house and fit it all in the back of your car is one of the great pleasures of the modern age. Unfortunately, assembling flatpack furniture has become one of the greatest challenges, but it can be done. If you adopt a positive, realistic approach, there is no reason why putting together a chest of drawers should not be an enjoyable task and even the highlight of your week.

take your time
The first rule is to allow plenty of time. It always takes longer than you think. Even though you cannot wait to transform the drawing on that slim box of parts into its three-dimensional form, don't think that you can do in those couple of hours between bringing it home and going out for the evening. Treat it as a pleasurable activity and plan a day around it: get in plenty of snacks, but avoid alcohol – save that for the celebration of a job well done or, in extreme circumstances, a good way of forgetting. Don't attempt it if you are feeling grumpy, and don't invite lots of people to help. Do get one other

person to help as two sets of arms and hands can be useful.

room for manoeuvre
Choose where the assembly will take place. Allow plenty of space, but if the piece of furniture is very large make sure you will be able to get it into the room it is destined for. Make sure you have the right tools. Some will be included with the kit but you may need screwdrivers, spanners and, if it is a particularly adventurous purchase, clamps.

take a count
Unpack carefully. Avoid tearing the cardboard box, keep it, open it out and use it to work on. It will protect the parts, and the floor, from accidental scratches. Examine all the pieces for damage. If they are damaged pack it all up again and take it back – annoying, but worth it in the end. If you are lucky there will be a list of components and a sheet of instructions so you can check everything is there. Identify each piece and make sure they look like those in the diagram. Make sure you understand what each piece is and what it is for. Count the

screws, bolts and fixings and make sure the numbers correspond with the numbers stated on the instructions. Sometimes extra screws are included – make sure you are aware of this in order to avoid the panic induced by the sight of two large screws glinting ominously alongside an apparently fully assembled piece of furniture.

stick to the plan
Lay everything out. Some pieces may look similar so to make sure you don't end up with something that is upside down or inside out, mark and identify each piece with useful phrases such as 'this way up' written on pieces of paper secured with removable tape. Next, follow the instructions. This sounds obvious and easy, but unfortunately isn't always the case. Some instruction sheets are notable by their absence while others require either a lot of imagination, the ability to speak a foreign language or an advanced qualification in technical drawing. Fortunately, things have improved and most good-quality flatpack comes with a fairly clear guide – or sometimes even a video! Even if you

think you know better, do things in the order it says – there is a usually a good reason. It is better to obey instructions otherwise you may be forced to take everything apart again just to fix one drawer runner or hinge.

don't panic

If things don't seem to be going too well, keep calm. Take a break and have a biscuit while you look through the instructions again. Don't force anything or assume that because holes nearly correspond they are the right ones in the right place. It is tempting to assume that a hole has been drilled in the wrong place but computerised mass production means that unless the robots were out for revenge, it is unlikely that a hole has been made where it shouldn't. However, manufacturing errors do occur, so if things don't make sense it is worth ringing the store where you bought it to check if they have had similar complaints. Mostly, things start to fit together nicely but be careful not to get carried away and ruin things by rushing. Check regularly that nothing has been left out and everything is the right way round and the

right way up. Don't tighten every screw or bolt immediately, in case you need to allow for some adjustment. Also, the instructions may specify in which order everything should be tightened.

final analysis

If at any time during the proceedings the object growing in front of you ceases to resemble the drawing on the box or instructions, or the photograph in the catalogue, then don't panic. Sometimes, the same instructions are used to cover a range of different designs. This is because the basic frame and components are similar, and the differences are in details such as colour, material or trimmings. It could be, however, that you have made a minor, or even major, mistake in your assembly. Go back to the instructions and, if necessary, take it all apart and start again, in which case, for the benefit of your own emotional state and to protect the potential piece of furniture, walk away from it for a while and start again when you are feeling better. If you still can't work it out, pack it all away neatly and phone a friend.

shelves made easy

Shelves are incredibly useful and in even the most well-equipped home there is always room for at least one more. Open shelves turn storage into display and can become an important component, or even the centrepiece, of an interior.

shelving considerations

The shelving system you choose will depend on the state of the wall on which you want your shelves and what you want to store. Partition walls will not be able to support heavy shelves or heavy loads unless you are able to screw the supports or brackets into the wooden studs. The walls of old properties may be too soft and crumbly to hold screws securely and drilling into stone is not easy. Some properties have concrete walls which require a very powerful drill for even the smallest jobs. If drilling into the wall is not an option you may decide to solve your shelving requirements with a free-standing system.

Aesthetics are also important – imaginative materials can turn simple components into a style statement. Shelves are most often made of wood since it is easy to cut to size and is available in many varieties, but glass and metal can also be used. Shelves are supported and fixed to the wall in a variety of ways including brackets, battens, slotted uprights and dowels. It is easy to assume that buying brackets and shelves separately is cheaper, but although the individual components are not expensive the combined cost can be higher than the price of a bookcase or ready-packaged system, so work out your sums before making a final decision.

shelving materials

DIY stores sell ready-made shelving in a variety of lengths, widths and finishes and will usually cut specified lengths free of charge. Wooden shelves left bare need treating and sealing to prevent them from drying out and distorting, and if they are to be painted they will need priming first.

solid wood

Softwoods such as pine are relatively inexpensive and can be stained and sealed or painted.

hardwood

Available from timber merchants hardwoods such as oak and beech look wonderful but are more expensive and heavier than other shelving materials.

laminated solid wood

Strips or blocks of solid wood glued together to form a knot-free surface suitable for sealing or painting; commercially known as prem-board.

plywood

Thin layers of wood sandwiched together and glued into sheets. Good for shelves, but should be cut by machine and the edges will need careful finishing.

laminated boards

Chipboard covered with laminates or veneers. Light, convenient and inexpensive.

metal

Stainless steel and wire mesh are great shelving materials but buy ready-cut and finished as they are difficult to work with.

glass

Use toughened glass and always get it cut and finished by a glass supplier.

off-the-peg shelving systems

Look out for ready-made shelves at DIY and interiors stores. With some shelving systems the shelves are often sold separately and can be used for convenience or to give a more prosaic shelving system a smarter look. There are a number of flexible shelving systems on the market which vary in price and complexity. The simplest consist of narrow metal uprights with slots or a single groove along their whole length into which purpose-made metal brackets are fitted. The choice of positions is wide and the brackets can be moved easily to adjust the height of the shelves.

off-the-shelf shelves

A variety of 'ready-to-hang' shelves are now available. Some incorporate extras such as hanging rails, plate racks, etc., while others are plain but made from more unusual materials such as wire mesh, stainless steel or plastic – materials that a DIYer would have difficulty working with. Most can be fixed directly to the wall with screws (which are often included, along with wall plugs) so require nothing more than a drill and a spirit level to put them up.

The floating shelf, one of the most popular of the 'ready-to-hang' varieties, is a box-like construction with a batten and bolt system which is entirely concealed within the construction so that the shelf 'floats' with no visible means of support. These look very smart and 'architectural' and can be surprisingly inexpensive. Putting them up involves screwing the batten to the wall and securing the shelf to the batten from underneath.

free-standing shelving

There are a variety of free-standing shelving systems around from very inexpensive wooden or metal units for garage or utility room storage to smarter combinations using high-quality materials. Most consist of uprights and shelves in a choice of height, width and depth and are usually very easy to assemble.

They are ideal if your walls are not suitable for fixing into, or you don't want or are not allowed to drill into them. Easy to take down and re-assemble in a different position according to need or whim they can also be used as room dividers. Inexpensive wooden systems are perfect as a temporary storage solution to keep everything under control while you plan more permanent or sophisticated fittings, but they can also be smartened up with stain or paint to suit the decor.

brackets

Simple brackets are screwed to the wall individually. The size and number of brackets required will depend on the length, depth and width of the shelf and its loadbearing requirements.

Pressed steel brackets are cheap and cheerful and can look very chic in a 'loft' sort of way. Look out for smarter designs in stainless steel and curved plywood. Cheaper brackets are sold singly but the more expensive versions are often sold in pairs.

They are ideal for a single shelf – use large, chunky brackets and a slab of wood as a feature, or use several brackets to support a long shelf which could even extend around the whole room.

Systems using brackets that slot into a metal upright, which is screwed into the wall, are flexible and involve less drilling.

putting up shelves

double measure

When fitting shelves inside alcoves take measurements at the back, the front and all the way down as the walls are rarely true. Unless you want an exact fit get all the shelves cut to the smallest measurement.

weight watching

To ensure good support when putting shelves on brackets make sure there is sufficient overhang each side of the brackets. The amount will depend on the thickness of the shelf and the weight of the load. Books are heavy and therefore you may need extra brackets and stout shelves to avoid sag or collapse. Most brackets have holes for screwing the bracket to the underside of the shelf. This strengthens the fixture and prevents the shelf from tipping or sliding.

on the level

Always use a spirit level for marking and positioning shelves so that they are level. Sloping walls and ceiling may make the shelf look 'out' but lining up with anything other than the true horizontal and vertical will lead to problems which are structural as well as visual.

You can never have too many shelves so put one up today!

shelves with brackets

The shelf is positioned so it overhangs the brackets at each end but will sag if either the brackets are too far apart or the shelf material is too thin or weak to support sufficient weight. The bracket should span nearly the whole depth of the shelf and, for heavy loads, the part of the bracket that fixes to the wall needs to be long enough to provide good support.

Mark the position of the shelf on the wall then work out the positions of the brackets allowing for the overhang. If you are using more than two brackets space them evenly along the length of the shelf, measuring from the centre for accuracy. Hold one bracket to the wall using a spirit level to ensure it is straight and mark the positions of the holes. Drill the holes and screw the bracket to the wall. Hold the

next bracket against the wall on its marked position. If you are using more than two brackets do the end ones first. Place the shelf across both brackets, place a spirit level on the shelf and adjust the position of the bracket until the shelf is level. Mark the position of the holes and fix as before.

flexible shelving systems

To work out where the uprights need to be positioned fix the first upright to the wall with the top screw only. Using a spirit level to ensure it is vertical, mark the positions of the other screws (see fig. 1). Next screw the first upright to the wall with the required number of screws. Insert a bracket near the top of the fixed upright and another in the corresponding position on the second un-fixed upright. Hold it where it is to be fixed to the wall. Place a shelf across the brackets and, using a spirit level, move the upright into the correct position, mark the top hole then fix as before (see fig. 2).

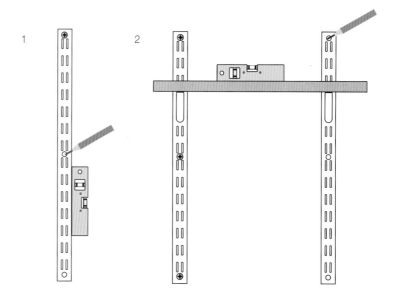

shelves for alcoves

shelves with battens

Where shelves span the entire area between two walls – such as in an alcove – they can be supported on battens screwed to the side walls. As the support is at the ends only, it is important to use a sufficiently strong shelf so it won't sag. The batten is cut shorter than the shelf and the front edge is chamfered (cut at an angle) so it is less visible. For wide spans and heavy loads extra support can be provided by adding another batten along the back, or a lipping of wood attached to the front edge of the shelf and batten, in which case the batten spans the full depth of the shelf.

Cut battens to the required length, sand the edges and chamfer the ends if they will show. Drill pilot holes right through, using a countersink to hide the screws. Work out the position of each shelf and mark the position of the battens on one wall only. Starting at the top, fix the first batten to the wall (see page 32) then place the shelf in position supported on the fixed batten and the un-fixed batten held against the wall on the other side. When you are satisfied the shelf is level, mark the position of the batten with a pencil line or with a bradawl poked through pre-drilled pilot holes.

An alternative to wood is extruded aluminium battening. The batten will normally be cut the full depth of the shelf and will therefore be visible at the front giving a neat, 'modern' feel. The fitting and suitability for heavy loads will vary according to the design and make.

angled batten shelving

Take the cut battens with pilot holes drilled through and, with a bradawl, mark the positioning according to the spacing you require between each shelf. Fix the battens on one side of the alcove only.

Place a loose shelf on the fixed battens and, using a spirit level to make sure the shelf is level, mark the position of the opposite battens.

fascia shelving

For a neat look fix a fascia along the front of shelves. Measure accurately the alcove depth then cut the battens and shelves short of the outside edge so when the fascia is added it is flush with the wall.

Attach the fascia with long panel pins tapping them well in so they can be concealed by filler before sealing or painting.

step 1 Use six castors for strength, mark their position accurately and don't put them too near the edges.

step 2 Screw the castors into position, check they move freely and the base is level. If the castor fixing is deeper than the base, screw blocks of wood to the base first.

daybed on castors

Furniture and storage which is moveable is convenient and practical as well as fun. Castors can be fixed to solid wood and laminates to make occasional tables and TV trolleys or attached to boxes and baskets for versatile storage. A wide range of castors is available, from large hospital trolley wheels to small spherical furniture gliders. Some are fixed by a flat plate with screw holes but many have a stem which screws or slots into a sleeve which is fitted into a drilled hole. Some have brackets to prevent an item rolling away at an inopportune moment.

A good-looking, strong daybed is simple to make using robust castors screwed to a solid-core fire door, which is strong enough to withstand a heavy weight and thick enough to hold the castors securely. Choose swivel-type castors that have a reasonably large wheel and preferably a rubber tyre.

castors Some castors have a flat plate which is screwed directly onto the base while others have a stem which requires a pre-drilled hole.

step 1 Drill pilot holes in the back panel ready for screws to fix it to the wall, then screw and glue it to the shelf for strength.

step 2 Place the lipping along the front of the shelf then pin and glue into place.

step 3 Fill over the pin heads, smooth surfaces and edges with abrasive paper and paint or stain before fixing in place on the wall.

picture shelf

Picture shelves allow you to change the arrangement of favourite artworks without peppering the wall with holes. Large pictures look stunning displayed in this way but the shelf will need to be strong and well supported. A securely fixed lipping or fascia must be provided to prevent the pictures from sliding off.

Cut three pieces of wood – a back panel, a shelf and front lipping. The dimensions of the shelf and the materials depends on the size and weight of the pictures. Using standard-sized battening makes the job simpler. For a shelf strong enough to hold pictures in frames, use a back that is no less than 19mm ($^3/_4$ inch) thick and 100–125mm (4–5 inches) wide. Make the shelf slightly narrower than the back and choose a fascia which overlaps both edges of the shelf providing extra structural strength as well as a ledge against which the pictures can rest.

10 ways with windows

How you treat your windows sets the scene, and the standard, for the rest of the room. Contemporary interiors maximise the impact of light and leave windows un-covered and un-cluttered with the use of blinds, shutters and simple panels.

bare if you dare

If you like the pared down look (and are not over-looked), leave your windows unadorned. If you value your privacy use etched glass or plastic film.

straight and narrow

Gathers are out. The newest curtains are simple panels, just a tad wider than the window, and hang straight from un-gathered tops.

venetian splendour

Slatted blinds in wood or metal look smart and very architectural. They can be adjusted to filter the light or block out the night, and pulled up out of the way in the day.

pole position

Hang curtains, panels, dhurries or throws from simple poles. Attach them with rings, ties, loops, clips or even safety pins. Keep it plain or add fancy finials for a little extravagance.

rings and things

Poles and wires are popular so rings are the thing. Choose from chunky wood, dull metal, shiny brass, cool steel and practical plastic. Keep tabs or ties on simple panels and try something out with clip-on rings or bulldog clips. Eyelets are cool and kitchen hooks are useful too.

the shutters are up

If you are fortunate enough to have original, old shutters you will know how they enhance the character of a home and allow you to control the light and the view. Ultra modern shutters are perfectly plain while slatted versions look pleasingly continental or a little colonial.

only natural

Bamboo and paper, unbleached cottons, coarse and crisp linens, hairy tweeds, felted wools, calico, sackcloth and crashes are naturally friendly (and terribly trendy).

great lengths

Cropped curtains are all the rage. No need to have them touching the cills or hovering just above the carpet; let them hang out half way between the window ledge and the floor.

along the wires

Metal tension wires are hardly visible and perfect for pared-down interiors. Use fine rings or special hooks to hang simple fabric, or perhaps paper panels.

on the rails

Sometimes good old curtain rail is the best for the job. It can bend round bays and hide behind pelmets, and some have cords for effortless pulling. A new type of rail has the track and gliders cunningly concealed inside a metal casing that looks like a pole.

guide to curtains, blinds and shutters

Most curtain fittings involve a pole or track fitted into, and supported by, brackets which are fixed to the wall or window frame with screws. Make sure the wall is suitable and that the screws are fixed firmly – the weight of the curtains plus the action of opening and closing them puts quite a strain on the fittings. If the wall is not suitable for screwing into you can screw directly into the window frame – but check that it is sound – and don't deface a beautiful window. Alternatively put up a batten and fix the brackets to this.

poles and finials

Poles are very popular and very easy to put up. Available in wide range of lengths, thicknesses, materials and finishes. Can be cut to size and corner sections are available for use in bay windows. The poles are supported by brackets or socket screwed to the wall. Finials are usually placed on the end of the pole as a form of decoration and to stop the pole slipping out of the bracket.

For small windows one length of pole and two brackets will be enough. For wide spans a third bracket in the middle is necessary to stop a single pole from sagging or to hide and support a join between two poles. Thicker poles and extra brackets may be necessary if the curtains are very heavy.

doubles

Brackets which carry two poles, or a pole and a wire, and rails which incorporate two tracks are neat ways of hanging two sets of window coverings.

rails

Rails are a traditional way of hanging curtains. The curtain is attached by hooks to gliders which move freely along the rail. The cheapest are simple strips of bendy plastic which fit into brackets screwed to the wall or the window frame and are suitable for novice DIYers. Smarter, more sophisticated versions are made from strong plastic or metal and the gliders are hidden behind a plain strip of aluminium or stainless steel. Some have the rail and gliders hidden within a casing. Rails can go round bends and corners and, as the brackets do not obstruct the rail, the curtains can be pulled right back. Also, the rails can overlap so that the curtains close properly to keep out light and draughts.

sockets

Where a pole spans the whole length between two walls, metal and wooden sockets which are fixed to the side walls provide a neat alternative to brackets. Ideal for inside window reveals and can also be used for shower curtains.

plastic telescopic rods

These are useful for hanging lightweight fabrics, such as net curtains, which can be threaded on rather than using clips or rings.

telescopic rods

Café rods are slim poles, often telescopic, intended for use with a half height 'cafe' curtain which can be attached with rings, clips or threaded onto the rod.

wires and cables

Wires and cables are becoming popular for hanging lightweight curtains or panels which are hung using eyelets, rings or clips. The cable must be very taut and is stretched between hooks or brackets with the use of tensioners.

Commercially produced systems include tensioners within neat bracket mechanisms but you can also make your own with cable grips, tensioners and wire available at most DIY stores or ironmongers.

Wires are often incorporated into double hanging systems along with a pole or rail.

mind the gap

Place the brackets far enough from the window frame to allow the curtains to be pulled right back from the window. Also, some rings take up a large amount of space.

The top of the curtains will hang a little below the pole so make sure the pole is high enough above the window frame so that the window and frame are covered.

When the pole is supported on a centre bracket the curtains won't quite close. Try putting the last ring a little way from the edge of the curtain so that there is a small overlap. If the curtain material is floppy sew, or insert some form of stiffening (a paperclip might do), to keep the edge straight.

hanging curtains

Attaching curtains to a pole or rail can be done in a variety of ways, some of them traditional and others inventive and unusual. Hooks, rings and other fastenings are often included with pre-packed rails and poles but many can be bought separately enabling you to create your own combinations to suit specific requirements and offering the opportunity for a little mix-and-match madness.

rings

Available in a variety of sizes and materials, from old-fashioned thin metal rings to flat stainless steel versions. Some have eyes, loops or hooks for attaching the curtain.

fabric tabs

Used to attach a curtain directly on to a pole or hook. Use cords and ribbons for something different. Look for separate tabs made from stiff materials which are fixed to the curtains through eyelets or fasteners.

hooks

Designed to slot through a heading tape hooks won't be seen. Plastic hooks are cheap and functional; metal ones are stronger. Use the old-fashioned variety for a retro look.

heading tapes

Sewn to the top edge of the curtains to provide slots for hooks and cords for gathering. Available with stiffening for deep pleated headings or double rows of slots for attaching linings.

clips

Often referred to as 'cafe clips' consisting of a ring or hook incorporating a clip which grips the curtain. Mostly used for light-weight fabrics.

eyelets

Bought as kits with tools for fixing, they are fitted at the top of a curtain and threaded directly onto poles, cables or hooks. Now available in large sizes suitable for heavier fabrics.

blinds

Blinds have traditionally been used in kitchens and bathrooms where curtains would be impractical, but with the vogue for simple, pared-down interiors they are now widely used for all rooms. The choice of ready-made blinds is now very wide and choice will depend on look, function, size, suitability and cost.

measuring and fitting blinds

size and fittings

Ready-made blinds are available in a range of widths and drop (length) and can be fitted inside window reveals or on the outside, depending on the style of window, method of fixing and the look you want. Try to accommodate the standard blind sizes by using a larger blind on a window where an overlap will not matter, or hanging a slightly smaller size inside a reveal with a gap at each side. If the window is wide consider using a number of narrow blinds in order to get the correct width, lessen the weight and to add interest. Many stores do offer a made-to-measure service, but accurate measurements are crucial – luckily most stores will do the measuring for you.

Blinds are usually sold complete with fixings, brackets, cord, rods and fitting instructions. Venetian and roller blinds are hung from brackets which can be screwed into the window frame, wall, ceiling or top of the window reveal. If you do not want to, or cannot, screw into the window frame, fix a batten flush with the edge of the frame and screw the fixings into that. A lot of strain is put on brackets so make sure screws are tightly secured.

sizing up

Blinds can hang in front of the window or inside a window reveal. When hanging in front the blind should be wider than the window frame (A). As long as the blind covers the bottom of the window the length of the 'drop' (B) need not be exact as it can be adjusted by cord or chain. To fit inside a window reveal getting a blind near to the exact width (C) is more crucial but the drop (D) can be adjusted as before.

fixing up

Blinds fitted to the outside of a window frame are normally fixed to the wall (A), but can also be fixed to the ceiling (B) if space is limited. Inside a reveal blinds can be fitted either above (C) or along the top of the window frame (D). They can also be fixed either at the top or sides of the reveal either flush against the window or at any point within the depth of the reveal.

types of blind

roller blinds

Attached to a wooden or metal rod and
pulled up and down by means of a cord.
A wooden batten slotted through the bottom
of the blind adds weight and rigidity. Kits
available for making your own.
Plus points: discreet, lightweight.

Venetian blinds

Horizontal slats held together by cord or
tape suspended from a 'box'. The blind can
be pulled up and down and the slats can be
opened and closed. Available ready-made
and made-to-measure.
Plus points: control and filter the light, screen
a view and provide privacy.

vertical blinds

Good for wide, floor-length windows. The
individual 'vanes' are hung from a track
screwed to the ceiling, or wall above the
window, and are linked at the bottom.
Plus points: a long drop, easier to open and
close than horizontal blinds.

Roman blinds

Combine the uncluttered look of a blind with
the softness of curtains. Available ready-
made and made-to-measure.
Plus points: choice of a huge variety of
fabrics, easy to sew, easy to fix.

other materials

Bamboo, reed, fibre and paper blinds are
lightweight and offer a quick and simple way
of providing privacy, filtering the light or
creating a mood.
Plus points: cheap and easy to put up.

Roman blind

Roman blinds are versatile and not too difficult to make. They look crisp and modern in plain white cotton, romantic in soft, translucent muslin or rich and luxurious in velvet. Lightweight blinds need only a cord but for heavier fabrics and a more structured look thin wooden slats are inserted into sewn pockets.

Roman blinds are attached to a batten fixed above the window. To make sure you have the right measurements for the blind, mark where the batten will be placed above the window before you cut your fabric. If the blind is to fit inside a window reveal the dimensions of the reveal will dictate the width of the batten. If it is to hang in front of the window frame allow for an overlap so the sides of the frame are covered when the blind is down.

Work out the finished size of the blind – the length will depend on its position and your personal preference. If you are using several colours, as here, sew the pieces of material together first. The width must allow for turning in along the sides.

The length comprises the length of the finished blind plus: an allowance for a turning at the bottom which is deep enough to take a wooden slat; an allowance for a turning at the top on which you can sew a length of touch-and-close tape; the depth of the slat pockets times two (the average number

of slats is four, which means you will need to add the depth of eight pockets).

Cut a similar sized piece of lining fabric and sew onto the panel turning in the sides, the top and the bottom but leaving the bottom corners unstiched so that a slat can be slotted in.

Divide the panel into sections from the bottom so that the slats will be placed at regular intervals up the blind, leaving a slightly smaller space between the top slat and the batten. Mark lines at these positions across the fabric with tailors chalk. Using each line as the centre of the fold, sew across the whole width of the blind to form a pocket wide enough to hold the wooden slat.

Press the blind flat and sew the touch-and-close tape along the top. Sew rings on each side of the blind at the top of each pocket. Attach screw eyelets to the underside of the batten to line up with the rings on the blind, plus one more to hold the pull cord. Tie one end of the cord to one of the bottom rings and thread it up through the other rings and the eyelets and back down to tie it to the other bottom ring, leaving enough cord at the top to pull the blind up and down.

The finished blind will look neater if you cover the batten that will be fixed to the wall with matching fabric before screwing in place. Staple a length of touch-and-close tape along the front of the batten to attach it to the blind.

step 1 Divide the panel into sections and mark the centre lines of the folds which will form the pockets for the slats.

step 2 Thread the cord through the rings and eyelets on the batten and insert the slats.

step 3 Cover a batten with fabric and staple a length of touch-and-close tape to the front. Screw in place above the window.

minimum exposure

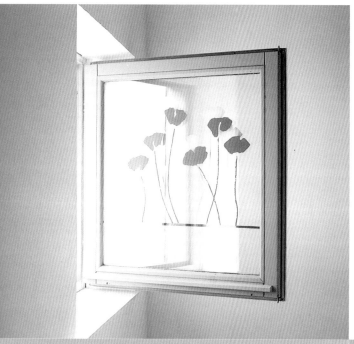

picture window
Use your creative talents and signwriters paint or specialist glass paints to turn a window into a work of art.

film review
Create the chic architectural look of etched glass using adhesive window film applied to clear windows.

frosty looks
There are several products which can be sprayed or painted onto windows to produce a frosty glass effect. Leave clear areas to highlight a view while maintaining privacy.

bare all
If you have beautiful windows and are not overlooked, eschew curtains or blinds in favour of the naked look.

under cover

mdf

Get plain MDF panels cut to size at the DIY store.
Fix them using shiny stainless steel hinges for a
modern look and paint them white or the same
colour as the wall.

off-the-peg

Ready-made doors for kitchen cupboards,
wardrobes, etc. come in a range of sizes and can
be used as shutters. Louvred doors are good as
they come in narrow sizes and are quite light.

fabric

Make lightweight shutters by stretching fabric onto
a frame or threading panels onto poles. Use screw
hooks and eyes to fix them.

serendipity

Be adventurous and use 'found' items for shutters
such as planks of weathered wood or the doors
from an old cupboard.

services with a smile

the basics on water, electricity and gas supplies

The services supplied direct to our homes – water, electricity and gas – provide us with the necessities of life as well as the convenience and comfort of hot water, light and central heating. Our homes contain complex networks of water pipes, eletrical wiring and gas pipes which are mostly hidden so that our only contact with them is at the socket or the tap. Connecting the supplies of water, electricity and gas to your home is the responsibility of the relevant water board or power companies. Likewise the installation and maintenance of fittings and appliances such as hot water systems and central heating boilers are subject to strict regulations. Any major work should always be carried out by a registered installer – failure to do so could affect any insurance claim should an accident occur. Never touch anything involving gas supply connection, the consequences of getting it wrong can be catastrophic. Always employ a professional who should be registered with CORGI (Council of Registered Gas Installers).

Keeping water in its place with good pipework and well sealed joints is a job for a qualified plumber but, in the event of a leak, knowing where the stop-cock is can avert disaster while waiting for him to arrive. We take electricity for granted and are mostly aware of its dangers, but sometimes, unknowingly, we take risks by over-loading a socket or using the wrong lightbulb. Understanding the relationship between watts, volts and amps will help avoid potential hazards.

Minor incidents such as a dripping tap or a blown fuse are irritating but not life-threatening and can be easily remedied, however, they can also be an indication of something wrong with the system or a worse problem elsewhere. If fuses or lightbulbs are frequently having to be replaced it could be due to a fault in the electrical wiring and if the sound of a dripping tap doesn't drive you mad the realisation that the drips have seeped through a poor seal and formed a large puddle elsewhere can make you very cross indeed.

It makes sense to be cautious when dealing with water and electricity so confine your DIY enthusiasms to the outside of taps, sockets and light fittings, leaving the complexities of water systems and electrical circuits to the appropriate expert plumber or electrician. However, there are many opportunities to improve your environment using some of the huge range of plug-in lighting and appliances, and it may be that the disappointing flow from your shower does not need an expensive plumbing job to rectify it but simply is a matter of screwing on a new shower head.

problems with your waterworks

Though not as inherently dangerous as gas or electricity, even a small amount of water in the wrong place can cause a huge amount of damage. A steady drip, undected over a period of time, can cause as much damage as a full scale flood so it pays to be alert and make sure that everything is sealed and watertight.

flooding

In case of a sudden and dramatic leakage, turn off the stopcock immediately. If the source of the leak is not immediately apparent (check any hoses haven't become disconnected) call a plumber.

stop valve or stopcock

A tap on the main pipe enables you to turn off the water supply in case of an emergency, or to carry out work on the system. It is important to know where the stop valve is. In most properties it is found where the supply enters your home, but the location varies and could be outside or even under the floor. There may be additional stopcocks so that water supply can be disconnected in selected areas such as a bathroom or the central heating system.

leaks

Small leaks can cause enormous damage to a home, especially if undetected for any length of time. Drips, damp or funny smells can indicate a leak so always investigate.

damaged pipes

Cracks occur in pipes for a variety of reasons including age, puncturing with a nail or freezing. Hairline cracks are difficult to detect and as the leaked water often travels along the outside of the pipe before dripping off, the location of the wet patch does not always coincide with the leak.

If accessible, repair the pipe temporarily by binding it with amalgam tape, a very sticky strong tape specifically made for the job. Hairline cracks can turn into large fissures so get it replaced by a plumber.

bad seals

Water can get through extremely small gaps; mastic seals around baths, sinks and basins are particularly vulnerable. Remove all traces of old mastic using a special solvent and replace, making sure that all surfaces are perfectly dry when applying.

Top tip: when sealing around a bath, fill it with water and leave until the mastic has set. If you don't, the weight of water and the bather will pull the mastic away from the wall and break the seal.

leaking joints

Joints and seals on pipework, waste pipes and connections to appliances are common sources of leaks. Areas behind bath panels, sinks, washing machines and dishwashers are particularly vulnerable so take a look from time to time.

Common causes are loose fittings, worn threads and worn washers. Try tightening everything up using a spanner if necessary (but don't force anything).

If water still escapes wind PTFE tape (a very thin plastic tape available from plumbers merchants and DIY stores) around the thread and re-tighten. Replace any washers and if the problem still persists replace the fittings or whole joint.

Hose connectors and plastic waste fittings are easy to do yourself but it is advisable to employ a plumber for metal pipework.

fixing a dripping tap

The most common reason for a tap to drip is a worn washer. Changing a washer is another classic of the DIY world and therefore no self-respecting, emancipated woman likes to admit to calling out a plumber for such an apparently simple task. There are, however, many different styles and designs of taps on the market. Some don't have washers and others are very difficult to get into – so don't feel a wimp if you do resort to using a plumber.

Modern taps may have ceramic discs or rubber O rings in place of washers. Ceramics discs are supposed to be maintenance free so should not need replacing. As the ceramic disc is incorporated into a cartridge, dealing with any problem will involve ordering a new one of the correct size for that specific tap. O rings can be relatively easy to replace. Examining the inside of your tap will determine whether it is possible to carry out any maintenance yourself – but remember to always turn off the water before unscrewing any tap!

If you have traditional taps (as illustrated) then changing a washer is not complicated. You may need to take the old washer to the DIY store in order to get the correct size replacement so don't decide to do it when all the shops are closed. If you are daunted by the inside workings and can't work out what is what seek the advice of an experienced DIYer or plumber who may recommend a new tap (which don't necessarily cost a fortune) if yours are old or of poor quality.

turn it off!

Turn off the water at the stop valve. Unscrew the cover and lift to reveal the 'head-gear' nut and unscrew it using a spanner.

Lift out the top section of the tap, remove the old washer and replace with a new one of the correct size.

going with the flow

Don't let unpleasant blockages interfere with the flow!

mains attraction

Most homes are connected to a mains water supply which enters the property through the household stopcock. Water is then distributed around the home via a system of a pipes to feed central heating systems, tanks, cisterns, taps and appliances such as washing machines and dishwashers.

If you have a direct system the water for all boilers, cisterns and taps is drawn directly from the mains. With an indirect stored-water system mains only some of the taps are connected directly to the mains. The remaining taps will be fed from cold-water storage tanks (usually situated in the roof space) which supply hot water tanks, boilers, cisterns, baths, showers and basins.

waste management

All waste is channelled to the main drainage system. Baths, showers, basins and washing machines drain eventually into a single pipe connected to the mains drainage, but the toilet is connected to a separate soil pipe. These two systems join up with the rainwater collection pipe and then all three are channelled via an inspection chamber (often referred to as a manhole) to the main drain.

quenching that thirst

Water from taps directly connected to the mains water supply is normally suitable for drinking. It is not advisable to drink water from storage tanks as it is not fresh and may contain impurities picked up from the tank or surroundings.

coping under pressure

Water pressure is normally good near to the mains but can be lost after it has been piped to upper storeys or stored, especially if the positioning of the storage tank means there is an insufficent head of water to provide a good flow.

If lack of pressure is a problem ask the advice of a good plumber who may suggest new pipework, the re-siting of water tanks or installing water pumps.

softening up

The quality of your local water can affect your supply. In hard water areas a build-up of limescale inside pipework, around taps and shower-heads can reduce the flow. There are several products on the market which remove or reduce the build-up of limescale. Always read the instructions as many are unsuitable for materials such as enamel.

There are several water-softening systems available and many people are choosing to put in a water-filtering system to improve the quality of drinking water. For advice and installation always use a reputable supplier.

Showers are particularly vulnerable to limescale and lack of water pressure both of which may improve by replacing the shower-head and the hose both of which are normally fixed with a simple screw fitting. A wide variety are available at DIY stores as well as plumber's merchants.

unblocking sinks and lavatories

Waste pipes leading from sinks, basins, lavatories and drains have a bend or trap where a small amount of trapped water prevents sewage odours entering the home. These traps are perfect places for blockages. Sinks and basins are normally fitted with a plastic trap with an access cap which can be unscrewed allowing blockages to be cleared. There may also be an access cap on the branch pipe (a straight run of pipe beyond the trap) and this can be cleared using a hooked wire – wire coat hangers are good for this!

However, there are lots of blockage-clearing products for putting down plugholes and lavatory pans that will fizz and foam to break down gloop, gunge and other unmentionable substances. Sometimes it takes more than one application.

Caustic soda is a highly efficient shifter of blockages but should be used with care. It is available over the counter as a powder which, when mixed with water, becomes alarmingly hot and steamy. Follow very carefully the instructions on the packaging, wear thick rubber gloves and don't inhale the fumes. All these products are potentially corrosive so keep them away from surfaces, clothes and skin.

If the problem persists this may indicate a more serious blockage further down the pipework – if you're unsure, call in that plumber!

sorting cisterns and ball-cocks

As with taps, the design of lavatory cisterns varies and many modern ones have dispensed with the traditional floating valve which has been used in the UK for many years. If the cistern isn't filling take the lid off (providing it is accessible) and if you do have a floating valve (also known as a ball-cock) check the connection to the float valve and make sure the float is attached to the float arm.

If the cistern is continuously filling check that the valve is working. If water is pouring out through the overflow check that the float is adjusted so that the level of water is below the overflow outlet. If water is continuously running into the cistern you may need a new siphon. Whether you deal with these problems yourself will depend on whether you can understand how your cistern works and whether any replacement parts are simple to obtain and replace. A chat with your friendly builder's merchant may bring enlightenment and a solution.

live wires

Electricity is potentially dangerous if not treated with respect and caution. We tend it take it for granted, only noticing it when something doesn't work or we have run out of sockets for our ever-expanding collection of electrical appliances.

Electricity is distributed around our homes along cables and wires which feed the electricity to sockets and light fittings. Amateurs are advised to leave any work involving the actual supply to professional electricians. However, awareness of the principles of electricity supply will help you use it responsibly and make you see the wisdom of leaving certain jobs to qualified electricians who know about these things.

short circuits

Electricity is supplied to individual homes through a cable to a consumer unit. From here power is distributed to all the separate circuits supplying lighting, sockets plus individual appliances such as cookers and immersion heaters.

Each circuit is connected to a circuit breaker which carries a fuse that blows if there is a fault such as overloading or a loose wire. Most modern circuit breakers are incorporated into a switch which is thrown when the fuse blows making it easy to identify which circuit has the problem as the switch will be in the 'off' position. When the problem has been identified and dealt with the switch can be switched back to the 'on' position.

Other types of fuse carriers have a fuse wire (which breaks and needs replacing before the power can be restored to the circuit) or a fuse cartridge. Replacing them is a simple operation but it is imperative that the fuse rating corresponds to the circuit and the correct fuse or gauge of wire is used. If you use a high rating fuse or wire on a low rating circuit the circuit would not know it was overloaded and the fuse wouldn't blow. Fuses are rated in amps: lighting circuits normally use 5-amp fuses, ring circuits use 20- or 30-amp fuses and certain appliances such as a shower unit may need a 45-amp fuse. A main switch on the consumer unit allows the electricity supply to be shut off whilst fuses are being replaced.

current conductor

Electricity is conducted along cables and flexes through a medium which is usually copper wire. The earth beneath our feet is also a very efficient conductor of electricity and any that escapes through exposed or unconnected wires will flow towards the ground, taking the shortest route and passing through any object in its way. If you happen to be touching that object, or are the object itself, the consequences range from a mild buzzing sensation to instant death.

It is for this reason an earth wire is included in wiring systems to channel wayward electric current to the earth via the incoming electricity supply cable. An earth fault will not necessarily cause the circuit to cut out and therefore it is still possible to get an electric shock, but earth leakage protection will break the circuit when any leakage passes through an outside conductor (which could be a person).

Earth leakage protection can be included in the consumer unit so the whole electricity supply throughout the home is protected. Otherwise it can be provided for individual appliances by using an earth leakage protection socket which plugs into the wall socket.

Metal water pipes, baths and radiators are all potential conductors of electricity and are connected to a separate earth wire which leads directly to the consumer unit and this should always be carried out by a qualified electrician.

Water is a very good conductor of electricity and great care should be taken not to mix the two. There are rules governing the positioning of electrical outlets in bathrooms and kitchens – which is why you have pull cord switches in a bathroom and no sockets or switches near to sinks. Always get a qualified electrician to carry out any work in these areas. Don't operate switches with wet hands and keep all appliances a safe distance from the water source. Never use an extension cable in a bathroom to plug in appliances such as heaters.

Warning! Do not switch circuits back on or replace fuses until the problem has been identified and dealt with. If in doubt as to what the fault is or the rating of the fuse, consult an electrician.

what's watt?

Plugs on computer equipment, stereo systems, radios and lamps are normally fitted with a 5-amp fuse.

Kettles, irons and hairdryers require a lot of power to produce heat so plugs should be fitted with a 13-amp fuse.

Cookers should always be connected to their own dedicated circuit with a socket and 30-amp fuse. Washing machines and refrigerators can be plugged into a normal socket with a 13-amp fuse.

Two simple sums enable you to work out the power needed to operate an appliance and the type of flex and fuse required.

Watts ÷ Volts = Amps (type of flex and fuse required)
Amps x Volts = Watts (power required to run appliance)

Trying to understand amps, volts and watts can tie your brain in knots but it is pretty obvious that a washing machine requires more power (watts) and therefore a higher flow of current (amps) than a lightbulb. It also follows that a washing machine needs to run from a higher powered circuit than lighting so the plug on a washing machine needs a higher amp fuse than the plug on a desk lamp.

Most sockets are 13 amps and, as the average washing machine needs 3.0 Kw (3,000 watts) of power, you can work out using the calculations that one socket will run one washing machine and the plug will need a 13-amp fuse. A table lamp with a 60-watt lightbulb will require less than 4 amps and so using an adaptor and running two lamps off the same socket will be okay.

Power hungry items such as cookers and immersion heaters are given their own circuits with their own fused connection unit able to cope with their high demand for energy. Information on wattage and amperage will be marked or printed on a label somewhere on the appliance and in the instructions, but it is not always easy to understand especially as they may also include different specifications relating to other countries in which the item is also sold.

Amateurs should not attempt any work on circuits, switches or outlets. Any dealings with electricity should be kept to outside a socket, leaving anything on the other side to a qualified electrician.

switched on

Know your plugs and prevent crossed wires, blown fuses and possible disasters.

wiring a plug

All new appliances now come ready supplied with a fused plug but knowing how to wire a plug is necessary for dealing with loose wires and blown fuses.

Most plugs have three terminals one each for the earth, neutral and live connections. The positioning of each is sometimes indicated by the letters E, N and L. The earth wire is normally at the top with the neutral on the left and the live on the right, but this is not always the case so if it isn't clear use a different plug.

To wire a plug, strip the plastic casing off the end of the wires using wire strippers or a sharp blade so the connector is in direct contact with the terminal. Bend over the ends to make them neat, solid and connect to the terminal. On clamp terminals the wire is wrapped around a threaded post and secured by a screw nut while on a post terminal the wire is poked into a hole and held in position by a screw. Check that the conductor is held securely.

Make sure the fuse in the plug is the correct rating for the appliance. Use a 3-amp fuse for appliances up to 720W and a 13-amp fuse for appliances between 720w and 3.0kW (3,000W). There are also 2-, 5- and 10-amp fuses but these are less often used. Don't use a higher amp fuse in a low amp appliance – if a fault occurs the fuse won't blow and a dangerous situation may arise.

Double insulated appliances must not be earthed and therefore the flex will be a twin sheathed type. It is still okay to use a standard plug and leave the earth terminal unconnected.

sorting out sockets

The number of appliances we plug into our electricity supply has increased enormously in recent years and few homes have enough sockets to take them all. In order to avoid dangerously over-loaded sockets it is both safer and more convenient to use trailing sockets which have a row of between two and six 13-amp socket outlets and plug into a single 13-amp wall socket.

Trailing sockets are ideal for items such as computers, printers and lamps which are relatively low wattage. Such sockets, however, should not be abused – it is better to get an electrician to put in extra sockets than risk overloading the circuit.

Power surges often occur in our electricity supply sometimes from faults on our own circuits but also occasionally in the supply from the electricity provider. Computers and other sensitive electronic equipment can be sensitive to such surges and so it is a good idea to use plugs or trailing sockets (or get an electrician to fit a special socket) fitted with a 'surge supressor'.

plugged in

The standard UK three-pin plug (left) is grounded using earth (green and yellow), neutral (blue) and live (brown) wires. A twin-sheathed flex is also used (right) which requires no earth connection.

The standard US three-pin plug (left) is grounded using earth (green), neutral (white) and live (black) wires. The US round cord plug (right) has no earth connection only neutral and live wires.

The two-pin unearthed plug is commonly used throughout Europe and is a sealed unit attached to the appliance. Other shapes and sizes are occasionally used.

Computer and entertainment equipment gets smarter all the time so need not detract from a stylish interior. Unless cables and flexes are kept under control they can look unsightly. How you deal with them can vary from hiding them away altogether, feeding them through specially designed cable covers or turning them into a feature.

Whatever you do, keep cables organised – labelled, if necessary, and accessible. Keep all wiring safe from accidental disconnection by feet, children and pets. The simplest way is to gather the wires together and tie them with plastic wire ties, string or even fancy ribbon. Screw cup hooks under a desk or table and loop them up out of sight and out of danger.

Flexible plastic sleeving is available through which several cables can be fed for a neat, businesslike look. Alternatively, fix panels to walls, table backs or desk legs to hide all cables and plugs. Place TVs and sound systems on lidded boxes or chests. Drill holes so any cables can be fed through and kept inside. Drill holes in shelves or use bracketed shelving systems with gaps at the back.

bright ideas

well hidden

Add light above a worktop or in an alcove using small low-voltage lights concealed behind a pelmet or batten. Use a kit – a set of lights each with its own connection which plugs into a transformer – which plugs into a wall socket. Look for short strip lights with a plug attached.

well washed

Use similar kits to produce washes of light up or down walls. Put them behind a pelmet (made from a length of wood screwed to battens) in an alcove or across the whole wall at ceiling height or eye level. Direct the light up or down or let it shine from behind or down edges.

Christmas all year round

Drape strings of small Christmas lights around a dressing table, above a bed or along a shelf for a gentle, twinkly effect.

surprise lights

Tiny bulbs set into flexible tubing can bring light to unexpected places – behind the sofa or in a bowl on a table. Hang them on the wall and turn them into works of art bending them into simple spirals.

bare necessity

For the pared-down modern look throw away the lampshade and use naked bulbs making the most of the wide range of shapes and sizes from large globes to tiny candles.

leading light

Careful or adventurous use of light can alter or enhance the ambience of an interior.

lighting the way

Putting in new light fittings can be fairly straightforward in terms of wiring. Other considerations, however, such as making holes in ceilings or walls, securing light fttings and working out the load on the circuit, make it a more complicated job best left to experienced DIYers or a qualified electrician.

There is now a wide range of different types of lighting that plugs into a wall socket so is much easier to install than connecting into the lighting circuit. As well as table lamps and work lights there are various spots, down lighters, strip lights and ropelights which can add mood and style as well as extra light.

watts and voltage

Several lights and lighting systems are low voltage (operating at 12 or 24 volts) and need a transformer to reduce the domestic supply from mains voltage (230 or 240 volts European standard) to the required lower voltage.

With reputable brands and high quality equipment the transformer is normally included with the fitting, either incorporated into the light fitting itself, the plug, a separate plug-in section on the flex or even into the lamp (bulb). If a separate transformer is needed then specifications and instructions on connection will be included. There are strict rules governing all lighting sold in Europe to ensure that it conforms to the requirements of safety standards as well as the electricity supply, so if you are tempted to buy inexpensive lights, or have bought something in another country, either make sure that they conform to these regulations, or don't buy them.

Many downlighter and track systems operate with low voltage lights so even though you are not installing it yourself, impress (and annoy) your electrician by checking that a transformer is incorporated into the system.

The world of lamps (lightbulbs) is complex and it is important not to exceed the recommended wattage as you could be overloading the circuit – take particular care with tracks or rows of spotlights and sets of downlighters. Information on maximum recommended wattage is printed on, or included in the instructions for most domestic lighting and now that there are several low voltage lamps on the market it is important to take note of the voltage bearing in mind that low voltage lamps can only be used with light fittings that have, or are connected to a transformer. Using a higher watt bulb in a fitting can cause damage from over-heating.

types of bulbs

Traditional tungsten lamps have bases with two types of fitting, the Bayonet Cap (BC) (left) or Edison Screw (ES) (right).

Reflector spotlight lamps are used for downlights and spotlights. Tungsten lamps are also available in a variety of shapes and sizes.

The compact fluorescent lamp (left) gives a bright light and is energy efficient. Halogen reflector lamps (right) are frequently used in downlighting systems as well as desk lamps.

domestic bliss

cleaning and caring for your home

A sure sign of being grown-up is a willingness to clean your bedroom without being issued with an ultimatum. Cleaning has become sexy and huge numbers of born-again cleaners are coming out of their well-ordered closets to proclaim the pleasures of household maintenance.

The therapeutic benefits of home maintenance include the cathartic effects of cleaning out a cupboard and the calming effects of a fashionably uncluttered environment. Venting your anger on the floor rather than a loved one can leave you, and the floor, feeling remarkably refreshed. Cleaning is a way of restoring order into your life as well as your home. Taking pleasure in simple daily tasks is very Zen, but it does put you in touch with possessions and surroundings reminding you how nice (or horrible) they are, and making you aware of the benefits of keeping them in good order (or throwing them out).

We know and appreciate the benefits of clean clothes yet often fail to impose similar standards of care and cleanliness on our environment. However, now that the style of our homes has become as important as what we wear, freshly laundered linens and a nicely ironed cushion cover can make us feel just as confident as a well-pressed suit and clean knickers. Apart from the obvious aesthetic advantages of a well-kept house the practical aspects are many. Not only will things look better if they are cleaned regularly they will also last longer. Caring for your house will not only save you money on maintenance and repairs but will help retain its value and make it easier to sell or let.

We are all more health-conscious nowadays and aware of the hazards of dust and pollutants in the atmosphere. Regular cleaning and good ventilation can often control and prevent allergies, and remember – it's not always food that gives us food poisoning it's often the dishcloth!

A clean, tidy room is more conducive to relaxation and if you value your home and appreciate the joys of interior decoration you will probably also enjoy cleaning. Even if you don't you may be able to turn it into a pleasurable activity by investing in a few gadgets and some of the many wonderful (and sometimes weird) products and potions available to make things easier, quicker and more fun. Our homes speak volumes about our personalities so if you want yours to say something nice it makes sense to look after it.

10 essential cleaning tools

Those already tuned-in to the pleasures of housework will cheerfully change their mops and dusters as often as their clothes, but even those who still consider cleaning a chore will find it hard to resist some of the new fashionable designs and colours now available in homeware departments.

broom

For sweeping up the fascinating collection of fluff, grit, dust and crumbs that are part of any normal interior. Soft bristles will gather the dust as well as the bits and will poke more easily into corners.

dustpan and brush

Essential not only for the collection and disposal of sweepings but also a safe way to gather up broken glass or china and nasties, such as pet poo or the odd dead mouse.

mop

You can get down on your hands and knees to clean a floor but using a mop and bucket is easier. For wet work the mops made from strips of cloth are best. A soft mop, used dry, is good for dusting floors.

bucket

Everyone needs a bucket at some time. Plastic is cheap and cheerful, but chic. Galvanised metal, stainless steel and white enamel are very designer but also heavy and noisy.

cloths and dusters

Whether you invest in the latest hi-tech duster or just use an old vest, a plentiful selection of cleaning cloths is as essential as a good supply of underwear. Use cotton dishcloths, fluffy dusters and linen scrim.

scrubbing brushes

There comes a time when a good old-fashioned scrub is the only way to get things clean. Choose from bristly, country wooden ones to the chic, modern cool of plastics.

scourers

Flat, nylon scourers (available on their own or stuck to a sponge) are good for cleaning pans, but are also great for scrubbing off built-up dirt and deposits. They are perfect for washing down paintwork in preparation for painting or just giving furniture or flower pots a good clean.

toothbrushes

There must be a hundred and one uses for an old toothbrush. Cleaning round the bases of taps, the corners of window frames and the crevices of ornaments are just three of them.

vacuum cleaner

A vacuum cleaner is the domestic equivalent of a best friend. It's the only really efficient way of removing dust and can be used for everything from floors to furniture.

sponges

Available in lots of shapes, sizes and compositions. Big foam sponges are fine for sloshing on lots of suds but not so good at mopping them up. More expensive, heavier ones are more absorbent and more efficient, while small, natural sponges used for make-up are great for cleaning delicate objects.

10 essential cleaning products

Bring a sparkle to your life with a few basic cleaning products.

spit and polish

The joys of housework are not obvious to everyone but few would deny the pleasures of a freshly cleaned room. Fussy fanatics may extol the virtues of daily dusting and vigorous vacuuming but hectic lives often dictate that precious time is spent waxing legs rather than floors. However, unless you are a complete slob, basic chores such as cleaning sinks and baths will need doing, but there is no mystique, and no need for a cupboard full of cleaning potions and lotions. A good vacuum cleaner, a plentiful supply of cloths and a few basic cleaning materials is all that is required. And once you have accepted that pristine perfection only exists in magazine interiors, the dreaded housework will seem less daunting and, who knows, even a delight.

There are vast numbers of cleaning products suitable for all sorts of cleaning tasks and problems, many of which you didn't realise you had! The good news is that while some of them are undoubtedly very efficient (and expensive) you can keep a perfectly clean house with just a few basics. Cleansers contain varying combinations of detergent (used to dissolve grease and dirt), abrasives (to cut through more stubborn layers) and disinfectant (to kill germs and sterilise). Over-zealous cleaning with strong, powerful cleansers can seriously damage your home so choose all-purpose cleaners which are usually mild and, unless stated on the label, will be suitable for most surfaces.

cream cleanser

Slightly abrasive but not harsh enough to damage smooth surfaces. Use on sinks, baths, loos and very grubby or stained worktops. Squeeze directly onto the surface and rub with a wet sponge, plastic scourer or cloth.

general-purpose floor and surface cleaner

Available in liquid form. Dissolve in warm water for mopping floors and washing worktops, kitchen surfaces and paintwork, or use neat for deeper dirt. It is non-abrasive and so ideal for wiping down cookers and appliances. Contains detergent which will dissolve grease as well as dirt.

window and glass cleaner

There are many theories on the best way to clean windows but a proprietary spray cleaner is the easiest. Several contain vinegar which adds to the cleaning power. Spray on and rub off with a soft cloth.

chlorine bleach

Chlorine-based liquid which kills germs and bleaches. Used for plugholes, sinks and loos and for sterilising worktops, equipment, etc. Use a weak solution for washing down or soaking and a stronger solution, or neat, for bleaching out stains.

mild soap and detergent

Useful for a good scrub or a gentle wash. Contain no harsh ingredients so are suitable for more delicate surfaces and as a frequent-wash cleaner. You can still get blocks of household soap which is mild and relatively free from added chemicals. Eco-friendly brands of washing-up liquid are also good and easier to use.

white vinegar

Good for removing scum and soap build-up from baths and showers. Use diluted in water to clean windows and mirrors. Will neutralise odours including pet accidents. Use with baking soda to make foaming home-made cleaners. It is acidic do don't use on porous surfaces such as grouting.

baking soda

Has abrasive and deodorising properties and is brilliant at removing stains. Can be used on clothes, carpets and wallpaper as well as stained teapots, vacuum flasks and casserole dishes. Dissolves grease and mineral deposits and makes a powerful cleanser for sinks when mixed with vinegar.

soda water

Keep a bottle handy for emergency action for spills on clothes and carpets. The fizz brings the stain to the surface so it can be blotted up.

lemon juice

A natural bleach and disinfectant. Use instead of bleach to remove stains on clothes, worktops and hands. However, use with caution and never allow it to come into contact with any form of stone as it literally burns the material and resulting stains and marks cannot be removed.

borax

A general-purpose cleaner that has been used for centuries. It is an important ingredient in alternative home-made cleansers. Not as corrosive as vinegar or lemon juice.

basic home care

Keep up appearances with the following surface treatments.

floors

Walking on floors causes damage – our feet efficiently grind in the dirt, grit and grime of everday life and gradually wear away the surface, so regular removal of these harmful substances will keep floors looking good as well as prolong their life.

A vaccum cleaner is the most effective way of removing dust and can be used on all floors (but don't use the beating type of vacuum cleaner on hard or shiny floors as it will scratch). Use the tools to suck up dust around edges and underneath things. Few people have the time (or the inclination) to vacuum every day so keep a broom, dusting mop or carpet sweeper handy for the big bits such as crumbs, spills and things brought in on the soles of shoes.

Dirt and grease can be removed from vinyl, concrete and ceramic floors by washing down with a proprietry floor cleaner (but for stone floors use soap). To prevent smears on very shiny tiles dry with an old towel or absorbent cloth.

Non-glazed tiles such as quarry tiles will absorb more dirt and may need an occasional good scrub using a slightly abrasive cleaner – don't use soap as it will leave a dull film.

The grout between the tiles can become dirty and stained – scrub periodically with detergent or an abrasive cleaner using a brush. Remove scuff marks and grease with a small amount of neat cleaner or white spirit on a cloth.

When mopping use a double bucket or two buckets, one with detergent or cleaner and the other with clean water. Rinse the mop in clean water after each wipe, otherwise you are re-distributing the dirt around the floor rather than cleaning it. Don't slosh water around and leave the surface as dry as possible by giving the mop a good squeeze.

Don't use water on wooden floors, although Polyurethane varnish or laminated floor finishes can be mopped or washed using warm water with a few drops of mild detergent and a very well-squeezed out cloth or mop. For waxed or oiled floors which are very beautiful and (usually) very precious, vacuum or dust frequently using a dusting mop

and only re-wax if the floor is dull or very dirty.

There are several products that offer protection, stain resistance, instant shine and several other tempting easycare opportunities. Use these with caution as they often build up over time into a coating that becomes dull, dirty and worn and takes a lot of effort to remove. Some floors may need sealing or re-sealing and old dirty floors can be re-juvenated using a range of special treatments and products. Always ask advice from a specialist – manufacturers often have a helpline and you could find yourself engaged in conversation with an enthusiastic, knowledgeable boffin who will recommend the correct product and treatment.

worktops

Worktops should be washed or wiped down frequently using a clean cloth. A solution of bleach will kill germs. Wooden worktops need occassional re-oiling, but you can dab sunflower oil on dry patches in between oilings. Never allow lemon juice to come into contact with stone – it burns into the surface.

tiles

Wall tiles can be washed down with almost any proprietry cleaner but a build-up of grease in kitchens and soap scum in bathrooms may require more effort.

Wiping down tiles daily after cooking or each shower or bath will prevent grease, soap and water deposits forming but this requires discipline (and can quite spoil the effects of a relaxing bath). For once it is a good idea to invest in special tile and grout cleaners and have a good clean when you feel the need.

windows and walls

Use a spray window-cleaner for glass and rub off with clean, lint-free cloths. If windows are very dirty wash them down with warm water and detergent first, dry thoroughly and then if they lack sparkle, follow up with spray cleaner.

You can remove marks from painted walls using a mild detergent and a sponge or cloth; however, this tends to remove the paint and leave a discoloured patch, re-painting the whole wall is often easier.

bathrooms

Even if you hate all housework you will want to keep sinks, basins, baths, showers and loos looking, and smelling, sweet. Don't go mad on the bleaches and disinfectants, it is much better for you, and the environment, to clean regularly. However, hard water causes limescale build-up so be prepared to resort to fizzy tablets in the loo and limescale remover for taps.

furniture

Furniture responds well to regular dusting, vacuuming and a bit of buffing up. A duster slightly dampened with a little water or spray cleaner will pick up dust efficiently and freshen up plastic and metal. Give wood an occasional polish with a good quality wax polish. A vaccum cleaner with a good set of tools is best for upholstery – the brush attachnment is brilliant for curtains and blinds.

electrical equipment

Electrical equipment such as computers, TV's, etc., attract dust via static electricity. Remove the dust frequently with a vacuum cleaner – the brush attachment can be used on keyboards – and you can also use a duster dampened with an anti-static cleaner. It is probably better not to use liquids around electrical items so it is worth investing in computer screen-cleaning wipes and specialist equipment cleaner.

10 handy housework hints

Whether you are a fanatical, furniture-polishing fuss-pot or a cheerfully slack sloven a few tips are always welcome to help get rid of the grubby patches, greasy splodges and nasty things that lurk in corners which are a product of normal life.

glove love

Use protection, dress for the part and really get stuck in. Gloves – rubber for wet work, fleecy lined for dusting – are essential for protecting those hands and nails. Buy yourself a special cleaning outfit – perhaps a huge printed shirt and a pair of brightly coloured joggers.

tapping in

For clean, shiny taps use tooth-paste (the cream type – gel won't work). Rub it on with your fingers and rinse well.

sweet feet

Buy several pairs of slippers for your guests to use – your friends will think you've gone dotty but who wants dirty feet on your newly cleaned floors?

shower power

Clean grubby plastic or metal-slatted blinds in the shower or bath using the shower attachment, a soft brush and mild detergent.

scented dusters

Sprinkle a few drops of lavender oil on a duster and spread perfume as you go.

eco deco

Go eco-friendly and make your own non-scratch cleanser by mixing 3/4 of a cup of baking soda with 1/4 cup of borax with enough washing-up liquid to form a smooth paste.

fizz whizz

Clean glass vases by filling with warm water and dropping in one or two denture tablets and allow to soak overnight.

tidy tools

Keep cleaning materials accessible in a nice box or basket to complement the decor – it will encourage you to use them more often.

shopping trips

Visit the cleaning department of a big store and be tempted by the array of crisp, checked cloths, deliciously soft dusters, prettily patterned gloves and brilliant gadgets and products.

clean machine

Don't forget to keep cleaning equipment clean – wash dusters and cloths after use, wash mop heads and brooms from time to time and empty the vacuum cleaner frequently.

stain removal

Accidents are inevitable, but tough stains can be tackled. Most spills respond to prompt action with mild detergent, chlorine bleach, soda water or a proprietary spot cleaner. Some products are unsuitable for certain materials, so check before using. Rust, mildew and damp patches can be an indication of a more serious problem; find out the cause before dealing with them.

Tea, coffee, red wine and cola can be removed with soda water. Mop up any excess, pour on soda water and soak up with clean rags. You shouldn't have to rub, but if you do always work from the outside in to avoid spreading the stain.

Treat discolouration with cream cleanser and bleach or various mixes of lemon juice, vinegar and bicarbonate of soda.

Keep a proprietary spot cleaner handy for difficult stains such as inkor dye, apply immediately and then follow instructions.

Tackle stains in stainless steel or porcelain sinks with cream cleanser or, if that fails, a solution of liquid chlorine bleach.

Wash out grease with mild detergent – eco-friendly washing-up liquid is gentle.

Wash mildew stains off walls with mild bleach solution, treat any discolouration with stain sealer before re-painting.

Remove stains and marks from wallpaper by rubbing them gently with white bread.

Scented flowers and plants not only smell wonderful but can look wonderful too. Seasonal flowers will help you keep in touch with the rhythm of nature's cycle.

Do not keep fruit in the fridge – a large bowl of apples can scent a whole room, especially if they are freshly picked. Gently browning bananas smell pleasantly sweet.

Keep linens smelling good with lavender oil or linen spray. Place muslin bags filled with lavender and rosemary between sheets. Add drops of lavender oil to pillows for a dreamy sleep.

Bunches of herbs hung in the kitchen will offer a subtle aroma while giving the impression that you are a keen and inspired cook.

Make your own deodorisers by sprinkling drops of vanilla or essential oils on to a cotton pad, refreshing when necessary.

Keep moths away with cedar wood and lavender rather than moth balls. Stores sell a variety of wooden shapes and sachets to hang in your wardrobe or place between clothes in drawers.

a breath of fresh air

There are many reasons for keeping the outside world at bay – noise, pollution and cold being the main ones, but though it is prudent to prevent expensively produced heat from escaping through badly fitting windows and doors it is unhealthy, and even dangerous, to seal yourself in too tightly. We are familiar with the concept of 'fresh air' being good for you, but we tend to associate it with spending time outdoors. In fact the air in our homes is constantly being changed and circulated, entering and leaving via specially fitted vents and venting systems as well as chimneys, open windows and doors and gaps around skirting boards, doors and windows. Ventilation is considered adequate when the air in our homes changes at least ten times per day – a surprising amount of air activity! Anything less than that and the build-up of pollutants in the air can be dangerous.

sick house syndrome

It is easy to get paranoid about fumes, fungi, viruses and other voc's (volatile organic compounds) convincing ourselves that we, and our houses, are 'sick'. But even if we lived in a mud hut and eschewed all 'dangerous' modern materials such as paint, cleaning products and cosmetics, the smoke of our wood fire and the straw on the roof expose us to equally harmful substances. However, by living in well-equipped, stylish homes we are probably surrounded by more noxious substances

than is good for us and we tend to increase any potential danger by cutting down on natural ventilation in order to conserve energy used in heating. Once you are aware of the need for air circulation it is relatively easy to ensure that windows are open (even a small opening is sufficient) throughout the house and that all vents are unblocked. Danger areas are kitchens where gas central heating boilers and cookers increase the amount of dangerous gases. There are strict health and safety regulations regarding the installation of vents so it is important to check that yours comply. If you are leasing, get proof that this has been done from your landlord. Lack of ventilation can make us feel drowsy, head-achey and generally unwell so before reaching for pills or the medical dictionary try opening a window.

humidity

It is not only pollutants in the air that make good ventilation essential, lack of air circulation increases humidity and therefore the risk of mildew and damp. Bathrooms and kitchens are particularly vulnerable. Opening windows to allow steam to escape is a simple way of keeping the atmosphere relatively dry, but if mildew or condensation persists it may be necessary to install a fan or extra vent. Not only is damp and mildew unsightly, and often smelly, it can do extensive damage to the structure of a property. Air needs to be able to circulate in hidden

areas, including the roof space and underneath floors, and over-zealous insulation and unsuitable floor-coverings can add to the problem. If you are experiencing damp problems in upstairs rooms get someone to check the roofspace and make sure that air is getting in and out. Before laying an impervious floor covering such as laminate or vinyl make sure that it will not prevent air circulating below the floor as this can lead to dry rot.

nice smells

Homes that smell nice are undoubtedly nicer to live in, but we can get carried away with inappropriate and invasive use of room fragrances. A clean, well-ventilated room shouldn't smell bad. If it does there may be a problem, e.g. damp, or something de-composing under the floorboards. We have become obsessed with smells and there are many products on the market that prey on our insecurities, offering us odour-free bathrooms and peach-scented sitting rooms. The perfumes in many of these products are artificially created using chemicals that only add to the pollution of the air rather than 'puryfying' it. It is wise to avoid aerosols, which are not eco-friendly and often contain unpleasant additives. Surrounding ourselves with heavy scents will desensitise our noses and prevent us from appreciating the subtler nuances of flowers, herbs, wood or freshly-laundered linens.

leave it to the experts

when and how to call in the professionals

Once you have experienced the thrill of Doing It Yourself, it is easy to get carried away and start planning other more ambitious projects. This is fine if the results of your first efforts surpassed your expectations both in ease of doing and quality of finish, and doing them revealed hitherto unsuspected talents you never dreamt you had. Graduating from putting up a shelf to installing a worktop, or from tiling a splashback to tiling a whole bathroom may only require one or two extra skills and a little more research, time and effort, so go ahead and plan. However, it may be that you found the work less enjoyable, easy and straightforward than you had hoped, and the finish not quite up to your high standards, in which case you are wise to limit your DIY activities to simple necessities such as putting up the odd coat hook and ready-made shelf. Either way, the experience and knowledge gained from Doing It Yourself will allow you to assess and acknowledge the extent or limits of your skills and so help to decide whether to tackle a job or call in a professional.

Understanding the complexities of the work will also enable you to appreciate not only the skills involved but also the time taken, and the costs. Major projects involving electricity, gas, water and structural alterations should always be left to a qualified professional who will be aware of any by-laws, planning laws, building regulations or legal requirements often involved with such work. Insurance claims can be affected, or invalidated, if work does not comply with strict regulations cited in the policies. If you live in a listed building or architectural gem permission may be necessary for any work carried out, and that work will be subjected to scrutiny by the various bodies as well as picky purists.

Don't subject yourself to the risks entailed in the use of high ladders, contact with electricity, gas or potentially dangerous equipment and materials, hazardous dust and toxic fumes. Anything that involves lifting or handling heavy wieghts or large volumes benefits from brawn as well as skill.

Doing It Yourself offers great satisfaction and enjoyment as well as the opportunity to save money, but don't be a martyr or feel you are letting down the sisterhood of emancipated women by admitting that you either hate, or just can't do certain jobs and end up calling in a 'man'. Lack of confidence and skill can lead to a poor or botched job which not only looks awful but can be costly to put right. It's far easier to admire someone for their level-headedness and level shelves than to sympathise with a do-it-all know-all with singed eyebrows and an incomplete set of fingers.

jobs best left to the professionals

Even if you have reluctantly 'called in the experts' the chances are that it won't be long before you begin to feel very relieved that you hadn't decided to Do It Yourself. If you are still not convinced, try lifting a bag of cement or wheeling a barrow full of rubble up a steeply sloping plank!

structural changes

Anything involving the structure of your home should always be referred to an expert as it can be unclear what is holding what up, and in extreme cases the removal of an apparently useless post can be disastrous.

It is often necessary to obtain planning or building regulation consent for relatively small jobs such as opening up a wall between two rooms. The foundations and the load-bearing properties of the structure must also be taken into consideration when contemplating new walls and floors, windows and heavy fittings such as cast iron baths.

An architect, engineer or surveyor will not only know about such things but can do any calculations relating to weight-bearing needed and also fill in the necessary (and complicated) forms for your application.

demolition work

Employ a builder for all demolition and re-building work. He can deal with unexpected discoveries such as wiring, pipework, structural faults and other hidden horrors.

specialist skills

Bricklayers, plasterers, carpenters, electricians, plumbers, painters and decorators all have the skills and knowledge to work efficiently, safely, speedily and with a high standard of quality and finish. Good craftsmen are expensive but worth it.

For historical properties you may need to employ specialists in a particular skill, material, method or process to achieve a professional result that complements your home and also complies with any regulations regarding listed buildings.

health hazards

Some building materials such as cement and insulation materials are hazardous or just downright unpleasant to handle. The dust and fumes from sanding, sawing, wood treatments, varnishes, paints and re-constituted wood are potential health hazards which you may not want to subject yourself to.

Dangerous jobs involving the use of long ladders, scaffolding or specialist equipment are also best left to professionals.

heavy work

Building materials can be heavy, large, long or unwieldy. Lengths of timber, sheets of plasterboard, MDF, plywood and rolls of carpet or vinyl won't fit in an average car and, even if you have them delivered, can be difficult to manoeuvre up stairs.

gas, electricity and water

Strict regulations cover the installation of gas, electricity and water. Failure to comply affects any claims on your insurance policy. Using a registered heating engineer, electrician or plumber will give you some redress should anything go wrong.

Apart from cleaning the cooker, never touch a gas appliance. Always use a registered engineer or plumber to install, repair or service central heating, hot water boilers or any other gas appliance. Use a CORGI (Council of Registered Gas Installers) registered installer.

Anything to do with electric circuits, re-wiring, new sockets or lighting systems should always be done by a qualified electrician.

getting the best from your handyman

Stories about builders are the staple of dinner party guests, newspaper columnists and comedians so it's not surprising that 'having the builders in' is viewed with fear and trepidation. It is never going to be great having your home turned upside down and taken over by strangers but there are things you can do to minimise the risks of trauma.

first, find your builder

Recommendation is best, preferably by a friend or architect – they are very fussy so unlikely to recommend a cowboy – but if you have to make the decision on your own look around your neighbourhood for current building works, take note of the state of the site (and the builders themselves) and if you are impressed, ask them to visit and quote for your work. Ask if you can look at a recent job and if possible speak to the previous clients.

the quote

Your new-found knowledge of DIY should help you understand, and appreciate, the complexities of a job. Before the builder arrives make a list of exactly what needs doing together with a plan or drawing if relevant. Inspect the site of the work with the builder so that you are both aware of all aspects involved in the job and any problems that may arise. Quotes can be based on an hourly rate plus materials or a single figure for the whole job (often there isn't a choice as builders usually work on one or the other). Make sure that the quote includes the cost of removing all rubbish and, if possible, an estimated cost of materials. Specify exact colours, materials and finishes to be used. Always get quotes in writing, preferably on the builders headed paper and double check to make sure everything is included.

Setting a completion date involves a mix of realism, fantasy and wishful thinking. Unforseen problems from the late delivery of a bath to the discovery of Roman remains can slow down progress, so be prepared to be patient. If you accept the un-written rule that any building work ends up costing twice as much and takes three times longer than the original estimates you will not feel too aggrieved when things don't always go according to plan.

terms of engagement

In order to avoid upsets and mis-understandings discuss methods of payment, tally of hours and materials, working times, access, storage of equipment, materials and rubbish, plus any rules you wish to impose. Establish how payment will be made. Some builders pay their labourers weekly and you may be asked for an advance of money for materials – but don't pay the last installment until the work is completed to your satisfaction.

Make sure they can store materials and equipment in a secured area and check that no rubbish or materials are obstructing public paths, roads or access for other occupants. If you live in a flat the other tenants they may not appreciate banging at 8am in the morning so ask them to start with quiet jobs or start later.

preparation

Clear everything possible from the area where work is to take place and protect surfaces – floors are especially vulnerable, with dust sheets, plastic sheeting etc. Lock away any valuables (front doors and windows are often open while work is being carried out), remove breakables and take down curtains and blinds.

It will be greatly appreciated if you provide a kettle, tea, milk, sugar and mugs plus the use of a lavatory and a never-ending supply of loo rolls.

safety

Good builders will employ good safety practices. Many choose not to wear masks or hard hats and secure their ladders, but while you may think this is their problem not yours, be warned! Recent changes in legislation have taken the responsibility for health and safety away from the contractor and conferred it on the client. The rules and regulations are complex so in order to avoid worries over liability for property and people ring your local health and safety advisor.

work in progress

If you are out during the day, inspect the day's work carefully each evening and note any poor workmanship, deviations from the specified job or materials. Ring at least once a day (but don't over-do it) and ask for a progress report. Give them your contact number at work so they can get in touch regarding any problems, choice of materials, etc. If you are at home, don't peer over their shoulder while they work. Keep an eagle eye on them in more subtle ways by taking them cups of tea and engaging in jolly joshing on the pleasures of good craftsmanship and the mysteries of why things never look perfectly straight to the untrained eye!

It is rare that a job is limited to the original brief. Extras arise through unseen problems or additional, 'while you're here can you just do...' works. Ask for a daily update on extra work undertaken including estimated additional cost in time, labour and materials.

good relations

You are employing builders because they can do things that you can't, so treat them with respect. It is surprising how many apparently mild-mannered people turn into demanding, snooty, unreasonable monsters when dealing with workmen. Builders are far more likely to do a decent job for a decent person who is pleasant and appreciative, so even if you have a legitimate grievance choose civilised negotiation rather than hysterical rant.

The common complaint about builders is that they take a long time to do things and always start the day with a cup of tea – but how long do you wait before your first cup of coffee at the office? Building work is physically demanding so it is unrealistic to expect them to keep going at top speed for eight hours a day and there will be times when they are waiting for things to dry, someone else to finish their job or deliveries to arrive.

They may leave early if they have come to the end of one job and there is not enough time to start the next and though this makes progress seem frustratingly slow consider how much of your working day you spend actually working between tea, coffee and lunch breaks, personal phone calls, chatting, gossiping or just daydreaming!

However, don't be too soft and don't put up with poor workmanship. Show that you expect some respect too, and that you know about building work despite being female. Most builders are men but don't play the helpless female, and don't flirt, this could lead to misunderstandings. Instead, show you mean business by being firm but fair and conducting yourself in a businesslike, but good-humoured, manner.

in your dreams

It's easy to be bitten by the Do It Yourself bug. Relaxing in your much-improved interior, sipping champagne to celebrate another job well done, all memories of dust and mess forgotten, you are enjoying the luxury of having shelves for your books and a hook on the back of the door for your dressing-gown, then, popping into the kitchen for a few nibbles, your newly-critical eyes are drawn to the ill-fitting cupboard door, the slightly chipped work-top, the inadequate storage, the dated design.... And before you know it, you have settled back on the sofa with the nibbles, another glass of fizz and a pile of interiors magazines, brochures and catalogues, and are busily planning a new kitchen which you will, of course, be installing all by yourself.

Of course we are allowed to dream, and sometimes, with patience, determination, energy and a healthy dose of down-to-earth, practical, common-sense, we can turn those dreams into reality. In DIY terms a little knowledge is a useful, rather than a dangerous, thing and if you are a dab hand at assembling flat-pack furniture and a whizz at drilling holes and putting up battens, then, in theory, you have all the skills necessary for putting in a new kitchen.

In practice, the classic nightmare experiences of wobbly walls, moving floors and falling ceilings can all-too-easily become the all-too-real stuff of a living horror story. However, using your newly-aquired knowledge of structural matters you should be able to assess and predict the possible pitfalls of embarking on such a project. Of course, once the champagne has worn off you may well see the sense of 'getting someone in'. And when you trip over the stepladder again on your way to bed it may set you dreaming about a nice shed in the garden, with a proper workbench, rows of tools and an impressive collection of equipment from power drills to saws and sanders.

Everyone dreams of having a shed, and just think, you could spend many happy hours there making pipe-racks and book-ends while the builder gets on with fitting your new kitchen!

Useful Addresses

DIY Superstores

B&Q
tel 0845 309 3099
www.b-and-q.co.uk

FOCUS DO IT ALL
tel 0800 436 436
www.focusdoitall.co.uk

HOMEBASE
tel 0845 300 1768
www.homebase.co.uk

WICKES
tel 0870 608 9001

Architectural Salvage and Reclamation

ARCHITECTURAL SALVAGE
www.salvoweb.com
architectural salvage and reclaimed building materials

LASSCO
Clergy House, Mark Street
London EC2A 4ER
tel 020 7749 9944
architectural salvage

WALCOT RECLAMATION LTD
108 Walcot Street
Bath, Avon BA1 5BG
tel 01225 444404

Bathrooms

IDEAL STANDARD
The Bathroom Works
National Avenue
Kingston Upon Hull HU5 4HS
tel 01482 346461
fax 01482 445886
www.ukcustomercare@aseur.com
special range of bathroom fittings for small spaces

Fabrics

DESIGNERS GUILD
275–277 Kings Road
London SW3 5EN
tel 020 7351 5775
cotton and wool fabrics, contemporary patterns, as well as wallpaper, modern furniture and accessories

NATURAL FABRIC COMPANY
Wessex Place
127 High Street
Hungerford
Berkshire RG17 0DL
tel 01488 684 002
plain linens, cotton weaves and ticking

NEISHA CROSLAND
137 Fulham Road
London SW3 6SD
tel 020 7589 4866
printed fabrics and wallpapers

Floors

CRUCIAL TRADING
PO Box 11
Duke Place
Kidderminster
Worcs DY10 2JR
tel 01562 820006
fax 01562 820030
www.crucial-trading.com
natural floor coverings, including coir, sisal, seagrass, jute and wool

DALSOUPLE
PO Box 140
Bridgwater
Somerset TA5 1HT
tel 01984 667233
fax 01984 667 366
www.dalsouple.com
rubber flooring, also suitable for work surfaces

(Fired Earth / Flooring)

FIRED EARTH
Twyford Mill, Oxford Road
Adderbury, Oxon OX17 3HP
tel 01295 812088
fax 01295 810832
www.firedearth.co.uk
wooden and stone flooring, tiles, paints, natural floor coverings and rugs

HARDWOOD FLOORING
COMPANY
146 West End Lane
London NW6 1SD
tel 020 7328 8481
range of natural woods

JOHNSON
H & R Johnson Tiles Limited
Highgate Tile Works
Tunstall
Stoke-on-Trent ST6 4JX
tel 01782 575 575
fax 01782 577377
www.johnson-tiles.com
ceramic floor and wall tiles

LITHOFIN
tel 01962 732126 for stockists
e-mail sales@lithofin.co.uk
products for protection and cleaning of ceramic tiles, stone and artificial stone

Kitchens

BULTHAUP KITCHENS
37 Wigmore Steet
London W1U 1PP
tel 020 7495 3663
fax 020 7495 0139
www.bulthaup.com

CRABTREE KITCHENS
The Sorting Office
17 Station Road
London SW13 0LF
tel 020 8392 6955
www.crabtreekitchens.co.uk

(Also at / Habitat / Ikea)

Also at:
Twickenham 020 8755 1121
Bristol 01179 292293
Dumfriesshire 01387 740288

HABITAT
tel 08456 010740 for
branches nationwide
www.habitat.net
modern furniture, kitchens, lighting and accessories

IKEA UK LTD
tel 020 8208 5600 for
branches nationwide
www.ikea.com
modern furniture, kitchens, lighting and accessories

Lighting and Furniture

AERO
96 Westbourne Grove
London W2 5RT
tel 020 7221 1950
www.aerofurniture.com
modern furniture, lighting and accessories

ALMA HOME
12–14 Greatorex Street
London E1 5NF
tel 020 7377 0762
fax 020 7375 2471
www.almahome.com
leather furnishings

CATH KIDSTON
8 Clarendon Cross
London W11 4PE
tel 020 7221 4000
plain painted furniture

THE CONRAN SHOP
tel 020 7589 7401 for
branches
www.conran.com
modern furniture, lighting, fabrics and accessories

DORPLAN ARCHITECTURAL
HARDWARE
434–436 Mutton Lane
Potters Bar
Hertfordshire EN6 3AT
tel 01707 647647
door furniture

GEOFFREY DRAYTON
85 Hampstead Road
London NW1 2PL
tel 020 7387 5840 for store
details
www.geoffrey-drayton.co.uk
modern furniture and
accessories

HEALS
196 Tottenham Court Road
London W1T 7LQ
tel 020 7636 1666 for
store details
www.heals.co.uk

INHOUSE
28 Howe Street, Edinburgh
tel 01315 525902
modern furniture and
accessories ·

ISOKON PLUS
Turnham Green Terrace Mews
London W4 1QU
tel 020 8994 0636
fax 020 8994 5635
www.isokonplus.com
classic and contemporary
furniture

LONDON LIGHTING COMPANY
135 Fulham Road
London SW3 6RT
tel 020 7589 3612
modern lighting

PALMA LILAC
tel 020 7912 0882
modern furniture, Perspex
shutters and accessories

PURVES & PURVES
220–224 Tottenham Court Road
London W1T 7QE
tel 020 7580 8223
www.purves.co.uk
modern furniture, lighting and
accessories

SELFRIDGES
Oxford Street
London W1A 1AB
tel 020 7629 1234
modern furniture, lighting and
accessories

SCP
135–139 Curtain Road
London EC2A 3BX
tel 020 7739 1869
fax 020 7729 4224
www.scp.co.uk
modern furniture, lighting and
accessories

SKK
34 Lexington Street
London W1F 0LH
tel 020 7434 4095
www.skk.net
modern lighting

VIADUCT
1–10 Summers Street
London EC1R 5BD
www.viaduct.com
modern furniture

Paints

DULUX
Dulux Advice Centre
tel 01753 550555 for
information and stockists
www.dulux.co.uk

FARROW AND BALL
Uddens Estate
Wimborne
Dorset BH21 7NL

tel 01202 876141 for
stockists nationwide
fax 01202 873793
www.farrow-ball.com

FIRED EARTH
Twyford Mill
Oxford Road
Adderbury
Oxon OX17 3HP
tel 01295 812088
fax 01295 810832
www.firedearth.co.uk
paint ranges by Kelly Hoppen
and Kevin McCloud

PAINT AND PAPER LIBRARY
5 Elystan Street
London SW3 3NT
tel 020 7823 7755
fax 020 7823 7766
www.paintlibrary.co.uk
paints and wallpapers by
Neisha Crosland, Emily
Todhunter, David Oliver and
Nina Campbell (paint only)

Planning

BUILDING CENTRE
26 Store Street
London WC1E 7BT
tel 09065 161136 (calls
charged at £1.50 per minute)
www.buildingcentre.co.uk

COUNCIL OF REGISTERED
GAS INSTALLERS (CORGI)
tel 08705 168111
www.shop.corgi_gas.com

ROYAL INSTITUTE OF BRITISH
ARCHITECTS (RIBA)
Client Services
66 Portland Place
London W1B 1AD
tel 020 7307 3700
fax 020 7436 9112
www.architecture.com

Storage

THE HOLDING COMPANY
243–245 Kings Road
London SW3 5EL
tel 020 7352 1600
storage specialists

MUJI
tel 020 7494 1197 for
stockists and mail order
modern Japanese storage
and stationery

Windows

JOHN LEWIS PARTNERSHIP
tel 020 7629 7711 for
branches nationwide
www.johnlewis.co.uk
wide range of curtain
fixtures, fabrics and ready-
made curtains

INFO WORKS
71 Bond Way
London SW8 1SQ
tel 020 7793 0677
fax 020 7793 0122
www.rosso-objekte.com
modern curtain fixing
systems

SILENT GLISS
Star Lane
Margate, Kent CT9 4EF
tel 01843 863571
fax 01843 864503
www.silentgliss.co.uk
modern blinds and window
coverings

Index

Author's Acknowledgements

Producing a book is very much a team effort so many thanks to the Quadrille team: to Jane O'Shea for asking me to do it; to Mary Evans for making me do things I thought I couldn't (and keeping everyone on their toes with her legendary attention to detail); to Lisa Pendreigh, the perfect editor who organised the text with a winning combination of good sense and humour; to Coralie, Jim and Katy, the book designers who used creativity and technological wizardry to make it all happen; and to Helen Lewis for art-directing great photography. And a special mention to Ernie and Michael who managed to make 'having the builders in' an enjoyable experience and also provided good advice and useful hints for the book.

Publisher's Acknowledgements

The publisher has made every effort to trace the copyright holders, architects and designer's featured in this book. We apologize in advance for any unintentional omission and would be pleased to insert the appropriate acknowledgement in any subsequent edition.

8–20 Graham Atkins Hughes; 25 © Elle Decoration/Neil Mersh/Amanda Smith; 34–39 Graham Atkins Hughes; 44 Sanoma Syndication/Dennis Brandsma; 49 Vega MG/Giulio Oriani/architect Elisabetta Pincherle/Studio 98; 50 IPC Syndication/© Living Etc./David Loftus; 56–62 Graham Atkins Hughes; 68 above The Interior Archive/Tim Beddow/designer Melissa Stephenson; 68 below Ray Main/Mainstream; 69 above Sanoma Syndication/Hotze Eisma; 69 below Taverne Agency/Hans Zeegers/production Olga Serrarens/www.greetedewilde.com; 70 Graham Atkins Hughes; 76 above Hotze Eisma; 76 below IPC Syndication/Janine Hosegood; 77 above David Hiscock; 77 below IPC Syndication/Janine Hosegood; 79 Graham Atkins Hughes; 82 Dominic Blackmore/designer Angela A'Court; 86 Graham Atkins Hughes; 94 © Résidences Décoration/Alain Sauvan; 95 Narratives/Jan Baldwin/bags by Somogyvari (helen@somogyvari.com); 97 The Interior Archive/Edina van der Wyck/designer Atlanta Bartlett; 100 Graham Atkins Hughes; 103 Red Cover/Winfried Heinze; 104–105 IPC Syndication/© Homes & Gardens/Geoffrey Young; 106 above Richard Foster; 106 below International Interiors/Paul Ryan/designers Kastrup & Sjunnesson; 107 above Hotze Eisma; 107 below International Interiors/Paul Ryan/designer Eugenie Voorhees; 108–135 Graham Atkins Hughes.